Celebrity
Bedroom Retreats

Celebrity
Bedroom Retreats

PROFESSIONAL DESIGNERS' SECRETS
FROM 40 Star Bedrooms

GLOUCESTER MASSACHUSETTS

ROCKPORT
PUBLISHERS

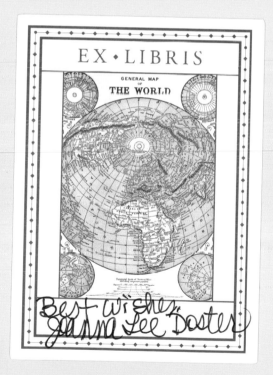

EX · LIBRIS

GENERAL MAP
OF
THE WORLD

Best Wishes,
Joanna Lee Doster

Joanna Lee Doster

First published in the United States of America by
Rockport Publishers, Inc.
33 Commercial Street
Gloucester, Massachusetts 01930-5089
Telephone: (978) 282-9590
Fax: (978) 283-2742
www.rockpub.com

Library of Congress Cataloging-in-Publication Data
Doster, Joanna Lee.
   Bedroom retreats : professional designer secrets for 40 celebrity
bedrooms / Joanna Lee Doster.
      p. cm.
   ISBN 1-56496-921-5 (hardcover)
   1. Bedrooms. 2. Interior decoration. 3. Celebrities—Homes and
haunts. I. Title.
NK2117.B4 D673 2002
747.7'7—dc21   2002004535

ISBN 1-56496-921-5

10 9 8 7 6 5 4 3 2 1

Design: Wilson Harvey
Production and Layout: Susan Raymond
Cover Image: © Dan Forer
Back Jacket Images: Mary E. Nichols/Ron Wilson, left;
   Anita Calero/Angel Sanchez, right

Printed in China

To my father, Jesse J. Dossick, who in his infinite wisdom has always encouraged me to embrace life, revere books, and reach for the stars.

Contents

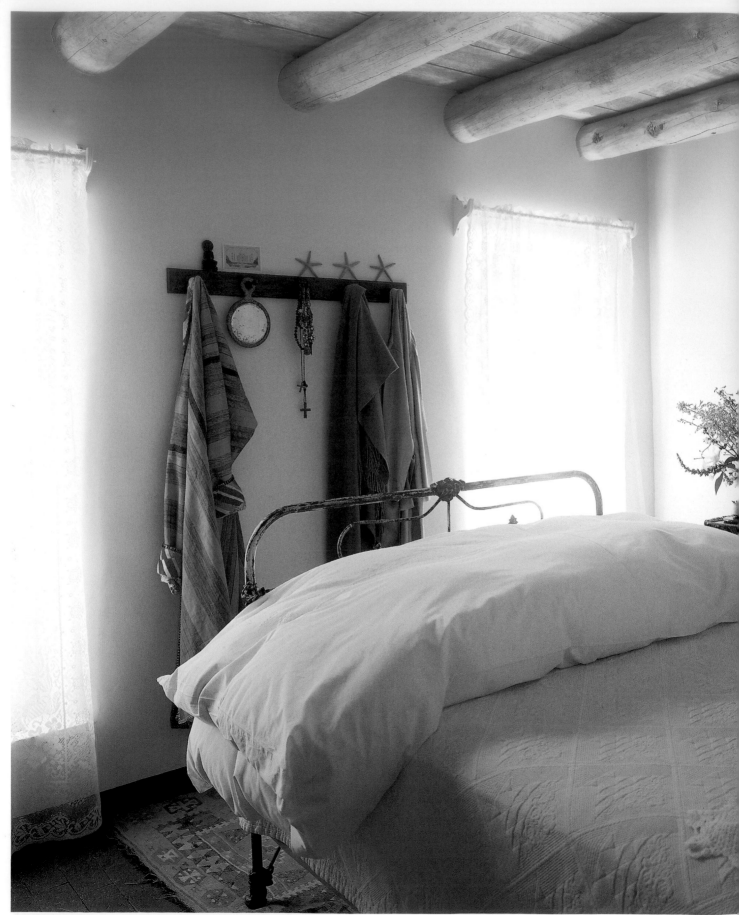

Introduction

Left: Ali MacGraw brings the
outdoors into her natural
enclave.

Below: Joan Rivers' romantic
spread.

Even as children, we have delighted in exploring the inner sanctum of other people's homes. A bedroom, particularly, tends to reflect a person's most intimate self. The bedroom is where we open our days, always full of promise and promises to fill, and it is where we close our evenings, wrapping ourselves in the true comforts of home. These comforts vary with our tastes, but they are unique to our well-being. We surround ourselves in our bedrooms with the things that we love most or that have the most personal meaning to us. When the big wide world seems a bit too much to handle, we retreat to the bedroom in search of respite for body and soul. This is no less true for celebrities—distinctive individuals from all walks of life—than it is for the rest of us. But it is very rare to get a glimpse of the private side of these very public people. That is the view offered in this book.

More than a tour of the bedrooms of the wealthy and the well-known, this book is a picture showcase for some of the world's most prominent modern designers, people who within their profession are celebrities in their own right. How a professional interior designer interprets the personality, personal needs, and desires of a celebrity client is not only fascinating but instructive to anyone wishing to create a bedroom sanctuary of their own. The strategies and materials described in the following pages not only have resulted in fascinating and beautiful rooms but can help inspire you to reach further and deeper to create more personal and meaningful designs in your own home.

Artistic Retreats

Artists—photographers, actors, sculptors, models, and even a TV sports hero—can be expected to have visually exciting bedroom spaces. What's often surprising is their choice of artwork to honor the most personal room in their homes. Treasured creations from friends and colleagues get pride of place in many of the bedrooms that follow; in others, the beauty of distant lands and fabled cities became the inspiration. From ancient nomadic designs to fine antiques and modern abstracts, the power of art to comfort and inspire shines through.

Above: Photographer Peter Vitale's display of art.

Left: Santo Versace's geometric retreat.

Art Deco Diva

AWARD-WINNING R&B SINGER PATTI LaBELLE IS
ALSO THE AUTHOR OF THREE BOOKS.

"We would spend many Saturday afternoons arranging accessories and artwork in the home or antique shopping—one of her favorite pastimes," says interior designer Michael Berman.

The many fans of singer Patti LaBelle will not be surprised to learn that this diva has an eye for design. The self-confessed owner of more than 3,000 pairs of shoes, she recently stepped into the role of shoe designer for a line of pumps that will be sold at Sears to fund WomenWork!, a charity that helps women "get on their feet" in the workplace. She has also released a new album (*When a Woman Loves*) and published a new book (*Patti's Pearls*)—all managed with the grace that is evident in her elegant home.

"When you first meet Patti LaBelle, you get this innate understanding that you might get from old friends," says her designer, Michael Berman. "Her warmth and hospitality are as genuine as her stage presence."

To decorate her West Coast bedroom, Berman was faced with a long but narrow bedroom, and a request from LaBelle to turn it into a "comfort zone"—a peaceful retreat for a busy singer and entertainer with a high-energy tour and performance schedule. Part of the answer was to change the room's dimensions—not in reality but in appearance. "We accentuated the apparent width and height of the space by focusing on a few specific items in the room," Berman says. "The Russian settee covered in white chenille helps to create the illusion of width, while the ivory silk shantung draperies frame the view of the Hollywood hills and add fullness and height."

Nouveau Meets Deco

Like Louis Comfort Tiffany, René Lalique began his career as a jeweler; unlike Tiffany, he made the jump from the sinuous style of Art Nouveau to the modern lines of Art Deco quickly. Frosted, incised, *pate de verre* and appliquéd glass, in abstract designs or highly stylized floral and figure motifs, epitomize his work, which was widely copied. Lalique's factories in France were also prolific, producing many small household items, such as ashtrays and perfume bottles commissioned by the fragrance houses Coty, Roger & Gallett, and Worth. Today a single vase or a collection of perfume bottles can evoke the essence of his luxurious style upon a tabletop.

The modern metal bed frame bisects this narrow room and lends an airy touch to the Art Deco era furniture.

The Design Details

BED AND BEDDING

The modern metal bed frame has a bronze finish and is draped with a decorative canopy of cotton gauze on the headboard side. The bed is dressed with plump white goose down pillows and duvet in crisp Egyptian cotton that has been given a damask trim. Hand-painted velvet pillows pick up the bronze and burnished gold around the room.

WINDOW TREATMENT

Floor-length silk shantung curtains are given a modern look with the addition of a boxy triple valance with pleated corners.

FURNITURE AND ACCESSORIES

LaBelle was a very active participant in selecting the Art Deco furnishings.

"She has an inherent passion for interior design," says Berman. "We would spend many Saturday afternoons arranging accessories and artwork in the home or antique shopping—one of her favorite pastimes."

Some results of this collaboration are the spoonback chair, which Berman re-upholstered in a cream-and-green striped satin; the large French oval mirror; and the Italian Murano glass table lamps. "I drew much of my inspiration for the interiors from her desire for subtle details, classic furnishings, and luxury in materials," says Berman.

The inspiration more than paid off, he adds. "The most satisfying part for me was placing the flowers, lighting the candles, and watching her face light up when she saw the space for the first time, and hearing her tell me that it's exactly the way she envisioned it."

LaBelle and Berman found this French mirror, with a patinated gold leaf finish, while antiquing around Los Angeles.

The Murano glass lamp was chosen specifically because of its warm golden effect, which matches well with the other gold accents in the room. While Murano glass has been treasured for centuries, the art glass most associated with Art Deco is Lalique.

What Makes the Look: Period Pieces

Quick, can you spot the Art Deco in this room? It's subtle, in a choice of forms, such as the curving dresser, and in the choice of materials, such as antique glass and the bronzed metal bed. This deliberate mix of decor in a variety of twentieth-century styles avoids a common mistake in Hollywood style interiors: going full steam for a period Art Deco room. It can be helpful to remember that the Art Deco movement (1920–1940) was a bridge between the ornate Europeanism of Art Nouveau, and the streamlined modernity that began in the Roaring 20s and has gained consistent ground in home design every since.

Decorative elements mixing silver and wood, such as the epergne, were common accents and often mass-produced. The travel clock, which appears to match, is of a different make but illustrates how easy it is to create a collection of Art Deco accents.

GIANNI VERSACE
DONATELLA VERSACE
SANTO VERSACE

A Legacy of Style

"The most important factor in designing someone's bedroom is that it needs to provide that certain person with his or her idea of a relaxed mood. For some, less is better, but for Gianni, more was what gave him peace," says interior designer J. Wallace Tutt III.

Gianni Versace's South Beach villa was only one of several homes owned and decorated by the vibrant couture designer. As befitted a prince of international style, the large, sprawling mansion was lavishly decorated in Italian neoclassical style to encompass a warm and close family circle that shared his vibrant home in America. His sister, Donatella, thirteen years his junior, started in the family business as a designer of accessories; his younger brother Santo, given responsibilities as CEO of Versace S.p.A., also had his own suite in the Miami mansion.

The renovation and redesign of this princely palace was placed in the hands of J. Wallace Tutt III, who supervised extensive remodeling that involved an extraordinary amount of luxury materials—and plenty of input from Versace himself. The bedrooms were designed as a set of private suites: one for Gianni Versace; one for his sister Donatella and her family; and one for his brother Santo. More than simply bedrooms, each suite was designed to be a private sanctuary to suit the personality of its occupant: Gianni's is imbued with deep, romantic color;

Donatella's is elegantly feminine, with many florals; Santo's has lively modern murals and a geometric rhythm as well.

"Gianni spent an inordinate amount of time in his suite," recalls Tutt. "Because of the time difference between the United States and Italy, he started his day early, in his robe, usually at the table in his dressing room. He spent several hours resting after lunch and most nights he was in bed by 10:00 P.M."

The vibrant colors, stained glass, fabrics, and murals used throughout the villa are typical of the Versace style, evocative of his love of life and his generous spirit, says Tutt.

"Versace used to say that he wanted his bedroom to be crazy and told our designers that 'when you think you have gone crazy enough with the design and mixtures of patterns and colors, go further and that's how I like it!' This bedroom is as flamboyant as he was," Tutt says.

Versace also wanted his Florida home to reflect the artistry of his Italian heritage, in a way that would epitomize the heights he strove to reach in American design.

Entry hall to Donatella's bathroom suite. She has used similar motifs, such as the stained-glass windows and painted murals, for her own home.

Opposite: Donatella's bedroom with painted ceiling. At the foot of the bed, a Directoire table (circa 1800) in ormolu-mounted mahogany supports an ormolu-and-mahogany pyramid box from the same period. The lamp by the bed was designed by Gianni Versace.

Right: The bedroom suite for Santo Versace features a geometric parquet floor and painted coffered ceilings. Bed linens are cotton satin duchesse in Versace's "Canova" pattern.

"While traveling in Italy with Gianni, visiting the villas outside of Venice, he admired the frescoes by Paolo Veronese at Villa Barbero, and said he wanted a modern adaptation of those frescoes for his own bedroom," says Tutt. "My office and Gianni worked with the Palm Beach artist Charles Segal for a fresh interpretation of the Veronese work."

The murals were painted on canvas, and then attached to the walls. On site, the artist painted around the seams to blend the edges together. Segal added palm trees and other tropical scenery and modern images to the murals. One of the faces of the musicians was of Gianni's companion, Antonio D'Amico.

The bedroom itself is an oval shape, with four curved, built-in cabinets, one in each corner, to match the Empire bed. These were designed with pocket doors, which slide away on hidden tracks to reveal the cabinet contents.

"Also, Gianni did not want to see any air-conditioning returns, or speakers on any walls in the house, especially in his bedroom," says Tutt. "Everything had to be hidden." So, crown moldings and even the baseboards got a bit of fluting to hide the HVAC vents and the speakers. The master bathroom evoked the majesty of ancient roman baths, with some modern touches like the double shower stall with gold-plated fixtures.

The juxtaposition of old and new world aesthetics posed some interesting structural problems for Tutt and his team. "Initially, Gianni did not want a television in his bedroom, and there were no plans for one," says Tutt. "But after the completion he realized he needed one." The logical place was in one of the four corner cabinets.

"This created a problem with the pocket doors," Tutt notes. "The curved cabinet doors had to open to reveal the television, but also slide back to be hidden. It's very difficult to do this with pocket doors that have a curve, since they cannot follow the track that retracts them. We had to brainstorm and designed a unique hinge mechanism to get the doors to retract."

The Design Details

PALETTE

Rich golds, Titian reds, and the deep blues and rich greens one finds in Italian Renaissance paintings are unrestrained and exuberant, used for murals, windows, and fabrics. Rich woods, often gilded and typical of the Empire style (early 1800s), punctuate and provide reference points amid the swirling color effects.

BED AND BEDDING

The bed in the master suite is ormolu and mahogany, an Empire style. Bed, pedestal cupboard, and two bookcases near the bed may be from the same suite, and all date to the first quarter of the nineteenth century. The bed linens were designed by Gianni Versace in patterns still available from his collections. Patterns on the bed are "Maxi Baroque"; the pillows and curtains are "Golden Vanitas."

OTHER FURNISHINGS

Versace's own fabrics were also used to upholster the armchair and its matching ottomans. Three different patterns were combined for a truly luxurious result: "Chinese Flute," "Chinese Gardens," and "The Mandarin." Art and accessories in this suite combined Empire-period art and antiques with personal favorites from the Versace line of home accessories, such as the set of four Neoclassical-style lamps in gilt and patinated metal.

THE OTHER ROOMS

Tutt's design team "burned the midnight oil" to complete the companion suites for Donatella and Santo. A pretty floral canopy was painted on her bedroom ceiling, and the walls are a simple, creamy white.

A master bathroom with double shower and a stone trough. The trough holds leopard-spotted bath towels designed by Gianni Versace.

The hall to the connecting bathroom was decorated and given a painted vaulted ceiling; marble and stained glass repeat greeny-gold and terra cotta accents throughout.

Santo's bedroom has a light touch as well. Trompe l'oeil was employed to decorate the coffered ceilings and modern art was mounted on the walls. The lighter furniture included Italian antiques from the neoclassical period and a pair of faux marble pedestals.

After Gianni Versace's death in 1997, the Miami mansion was sold and its furnishings dispersed to family, friends, and collectors who would treasure a part of the magic of this legendary style genius. In interior design circles, the South Beach house became its own legend, and is considered today a high-water mark that epitomized the peak of late twentieth-century home fashion.

What Makes the Look: Enduring Exuberance

Generous spirit, generous use of color, and exuberant style may be qualities that some people are born with, yet others can aspire and be inspired by a unique vision. Part of the Versace legacy remains, in the fabric patterns and home accessories that are still available through the Versace Home Collection.

Gianni Versace's master bedroom, with contemporary murals as a backdrop to a French painting (1822–23) by Sophie Rude. The painting depicts the sea nymph Peirine mourning the death of her son, Cenchirias, who has been accidentally killed by Diana, goddess of the Moon. The murals are by Palm Beach artist Charles Segal.

Tonal Textures

LILLIAN VERNON STARTED HER EPONYMOUS
MAIL-ORDER CATALOG BUSINESS IN 1951;
THE COMPANY IS NOW TRADED ON THE NYSE
AND HANDLES SALES OF OVER $200 MILLION
IN HOUSEHOLD FASHION PRODUCTS. SHE IS
STILL CHAIRMAN OF THE BOARD AND ITS CHIEF
EXECUTIVE OFFICER.

"Her home is her place to look at just a few special objects and give her eyes and brain a rest," says interior designer George Constant.

Lillian Vernon's bedroom is the antithesis of her direct-mail catalogs, which are jam-packed with all sorts of products to organize and decorate a home. But that "jam-packed" effect is exactly what Vernon didn't want in her New York bedroom, according to designer George Constant.

"Simplicity—it had to be serene and visually uncluttered," he says. "In her business, she is used to dealing with hundreds of objects and many people. Her home is her place to look at just a few special objects and give her eyes and brain a rest."

Constant worked under an uncommon restraint. Vernon "basically did not want a lot of color," he says. "I wanted the room to be very interesting, but still have the monochromatic feel for her. So I used woven and visual textures in fabrics, rugs, and details to make it an interesting space."

Two highly architectural elements stand out in a room that Constant says "is very long and very boxy and was originally very dark and boring." Opposite to the bed, there are two simple, woven panel screens that soften the corners and gently wrap a space for a low modern sofa, table, and two petite slipper chairs. The two screens are also a framing device for an unusual trompe l'oeil panel. It is a 250-year-old Italian painting that is a precise study of a stone carving from an even more ancient architectural period. Viewed from the bed, it gives an uncommon sense of depth to the far wall.

Among the muted, soft, and soothing colors, a few small and well-selected objects seem to glow like treasured jewels. All the furnishings reflect Vernon's extremely precise and orderly personality—notice the six vases precisely lined up on the sofa table.

Left: The soft monochromatic color scheme matches a beige velvet coverlet to the wall and is accented with pillows in crisp white linen and pale patterned silk.

Below: A long, boxy bedroom becomes a serene retreat when textured fabrics are used on floor-to-ceiling screens that soften two corners and frame a cozy sitting area. The monochrome panel is an eighteenth-century Italian trompe l'oeil painting of an architectural detail; the feminine design on the bright silk pillow is based on a nineteenth-century portrait. Recessed ceiling spots and the standing lamp in the corner create soft patterns of light and dark areas that vary the hues of beige and tan used throughout the room.

What Makes the Look: Adding a Sitting Area

Vernon's peaceful companions in the bedroom sitting area are the two petite slipper chairs in a contemporary nubby fabric. Their narrow width fits perfectly into the scale of this narrow, boxy room and could not be matched by bulky armchairs.

To achieve the same scale and the same modern look, consider using the small padded style of chair that is typically designed to front a dressing table, or use a pair of slipcovered dining room chairs. (For more formal bedrooms, or in period rooms, look for upholstered slipper chairs in nineteenth-century English Regency and Edwardian styles.) Small desk chairs that have armrests might be dressed up with fabric or leather cushions for a man's bedroom.

The furnishings at this end of the bedroom are not just pretty but are inviting for visitors as well. Guests can put their things on well-placed low tables, and rest their feet on the colorful deep pile of the area rug. Using a single lamp here creates an intimate pool of light that's conducive to soft conversations.

FROM JOANNA'S JOURNAL
Monochromic looks can go beyond basic white and beige. Pale blues, paler greens, grayed mauves, and seashell shades of pink may be arrayed for a soothing single-color bedroom. Use slight variations in the tone for walls, bedding, ceilings, and upholstery fabrics, and rely on textured materials to define physical shapes of the furnishings in the room. Imagine your favorite color, then think velvet, duck, cotton voile, wicker, wool, or matelassé.

CHARLES SHAUGHNESSY

Home as Castle

ACTOR CHARLES SHAUGHNESSY STUDIED LAW AT CAMBRIDGE BEFORE BECOMING A REGULAR ON BRITISH AND AMERICAN TELEVISION.

"[The bed] was inspired by an antique pencil post design, but made to be more chunky and hand-chiseled," says interior designer Melissa Partridge.

When actor Charles Shaughnessy and his actor wife, Susan, decided to build their Santa Monica house in a Mediterranean style, he told the architect, Eric Parlee, "Build me a house that looks like it was built by an artist, but with an axe." Interior designer Melissa Partridge was brought in at the blueprint stage to create the custom furniture—and the finishing touches—that would further this intent. The resulting bedroom has a touch of the castle about it—down to the sumptuous fabrics and a balustrade balcony.

The British-born Shaughnessy, best known in the United States for his long-running roles in *The Nanny* and *Days of Our Lives*, has over the years collected art and antiques and more than a little of that Hollywood style. Says Partridge, "I was a little afraid we might have some problems when they had a feng shui expert

look at the space, who recommended drapes to cover the open archway, and a fountain over the fireplace." She was able to convince them to move the fountain outdoors, and placed a pretty antique mirror over the mantel to channel the chi.

Since the Shaughnessys also have two young daughters, they requested decor that could stand up to active play, as well as a few quiet spaces to relax a deux. Partridge responded with tapestry-like bedroom seating that is made of a tough chenille, a Hatteras hammock for the balcony, and a low, looped "Pebbletex" pile carpeting for the floors. Just off the bedroom, the luxurious master bath features an extra-large tub with Italian tile surround, his-and-hers vanities, a small refrigerator, and its own stereo system.

Above: Elegant old-world fabrics and antiques suit this actor.

Right: The old-world fabrics were collected from a number of West Coast sources to create a European feeling in this Santa Monica bedroom.

The Design Details

PALETTE

The golden sheen of polished limestone, so typical of old Italian villas, was used for flooring in the master bath and other parts of the home, and is repeated in the glazed wall treatments. Partridge took her cue from the green-gold of an antique tapestry when selecting the luxurious fabrics for the bedroom furniture.

THE BED AND BEDDING

The bed is custom made by Partridge Designs. "It was inspired by an antique pencil post design, but made to be more chunky and hand-chiseled," says Partridge. She also designed the bed coverings and shams in damask chenille, scouring several Los Angeles suppliers to find the perfect bullion trim and pillow moss to make the smaller pillows.

FURNISHINGS

The rest of the room is a mix of the Shaughnessy's own antiques, such as the heirloom armoire by the fireplace, and custom-made pieces by Partridge such as the nightstands, "which were copied from antiques." She also designed the beautiful wall sconces that drip big crystals and have twin candlelight shades.

With terra cotta and polished limestone, the master bath recalls an Italian villa and has a bathtub big enough for two.

Bedding and pillows in a luxurious damask chenille take their color cues from the antique tapestry above the bed.

What Makes the Look: Fabric Interplay

The rich fabric treatments of the bed take their cue from the antique tapestry over the headboard. Heavily worked, deeply piled, and tufted, tapestry fabrics add dimension and texture to interiors. Partridge has used them selectively, on the custom bed throw pillows, where their lush chunkiness can be best experienced at close range. The thick fringe ("pillow moss" in the trade) is a perfect example of how luxury in small doses can be very effective.

Tapestry style fabrics are also warm, sturdy, touchable, and huggable. In this room they range from the elegance of damask chenille on the bedcover to the practicality of cotton chenille on the armchairs.

Other fabrics and furnishings in the room have a similar substantial and weighty feel. Window draperies are a heavy, stubbed damask. Chairs, nightstands, and the tall, carved wooden armoire create the feeling of a European castle. Even the custom wall lamps use big, chunky chandelier drops, not tiny ones.

FROM JOANNA'S JOURNAL
Tapestries and tapestry fragments can be found in shops that specialize in antique fabrics or oriental rugs (Shaughnessy's came from Aga John Oriental Rugs in Los Angeles). Fragments too small for wall decor can be made into bed pillows. Look for glass drops (chandelier fragments) and old-world architectural details (wooden finials, iron grates, carved limestone bits) at flea markets and use them to make distinctive lamps or wall decorations.

PETER VITALE IS A LEADING PHOTOGRAPHER OF INTERIORS, WHOSE WORK APPEARS FREQUENTLY IN BOOKS, AS WELL AS IN *ARCHITECTURAL DIGEST* AND OTHER MAGAZINES.

PETER VITALE

Personal View

"Since the bedroom is my personal retreat, I felt it would be an appropriate place to display my collection," says interior designer Peter Vitale.

Peter Vitale is a world-renowned photographer of interiors for books and magazines such as *Architectural Digest*. Having had the benefit of observing the work of many interior designers, he took a very professional and yet very personal approach to designing the bedroom of his home in New Mexico.

"In Santa Fe, one must always work with the *vigas*, the ceiling beams, for they are a dominant design element," Vitale says. "I chose an antique wooden door for the headboard to echo the natural wood motif." Then, for contrast, he added a pair of smoothly lacquered bedside tables and a lacquered chest. "The idea was to mix antique and contemporary elements, hard and soft materials, to achieve a quality that is modern yet timeless," says Vitale.

Both the bed and the room are oriented outward, taking in the desert landscape views through a large picture window and a door that leads onto a small deck. But the bedroom's real focus is the array of artworks, particularly photographs. These are not his own, but works "done by friends whose aesthetic I admire," Vitale notes. "Since the bedroom is my personal retreat, I felt it would be an appropriate place to display my collection."

Vitale also enjoyed working out the aesthetic challenges in the room. "There were several large heating-vent holes smack in the middle of the wall where the bed now sits." The solution was to break through the wall, lower the vents to floor level, and then re-plaster the wall. And because he was warned that the room's corner fireplace was dangerous because of its configuration, he decided to use it to display his pottery collection.

Dark-trimmed linens have "frames" to match those above the headboard. The figure photographs are by New York artist Salvatore Baiano.

The Design Details

PALETTE

Black and white and tan, but with a difference: The collected artworks truly inspire this bedroom, for the creamy white walls and sepia-toned dark tables complement the fine art photography in nearly exact shadings. A slight reddish glint to the wooden *vigas* and headboard are in tune with the ochre figure drawings and collection of clay pottery.

BED AND BEDDING

Vitale designed and built the platform bed, which uses a old wooden door for its headboard. "The bed platform has a good deal of storage in the drawer space below," he points out. "I spray-painted it myself in a textured tan color to complement the neutrals I prefer." Authentic Native American blankets and a down throw protect against the chill of desert winters.

FURNISHINGS

The smaller items, many of them artist-made such as the side chair by T. H. Robsjohn-Gibbings, came from previous homes. "I have had many for a long time and never tire of them. I identify strongly with the pieces I collect," says Vitale.

For functional furniture, he turned to built-ins. The bed's lower drawers provide ample storage, and a local craftsman, John Swann, designed and built a special photography desk in an alcove. The top is a smooth white ash, and a section of it lifts up to access a light box for viewing negatives and transparencies. When not in use, the lid serves as a desktop.

"There is enough room to add either a sofa or a large table, and I am still debating the choice," Vitale says. "I'm inclined to the table for practical purposes—for books and personal photographs—although the softness of an upholstered piece might be a better decorative effect. But how many people do you know who sit on a sofa in their bedroom?"

As a collector and artist, Vitale is drawn to the human figure as well as fine furniture. This male nude, by the late Santa Fe artist Dick Mason, is well complemented by the choice of a black fabric shade for the lamp.

The side chair was designed by T. H. Robsjohn-Gibbings; the four ochre figure studies are by Santa Fe artist John Fincher.

What Makes the Look: Decorating with Collected Art

Collected artworks benefit from an artful placement and attention to a few tiny, nearby details. Two groupings stand out: the four black-and-white nude photographs, their black frames echoed by the dark-bordered bed linens and rectangular design of the blanket spread (the linen finish on the walls matches the glossy photographic paper); and the four ochre drawings with their light wood frames. Pottery and earth-toned furniture integrate these into the mostly black-and-white decor.

The black-and-white "tiger" rug and black fabric shades on the table lamps repeat the color themes. The dark shade is especially effective with the charcoal nude drawing over the bureau. All these details unify the collection.

FROM JOANNA'S JOURNAL
Peter's collection of artworks also has a single unifying theme: the human form, whether it's represented by a sculpture, drawing, or photography. Multiple works from the same artist have been geometrically hung. While a single, large artwork—either vertical or horizontal—would also be effective on a wall, these groupings of smaller framed works, with a subject matter best viewed close up, provide the intimate scale that is more desirable in a bedroom retreat.

Desert
Beauty

TACTILE AND TOUCHABLE BRONZE ARTWORKS BY
GLENNA GOODACRE OFTEN INVOLVE THE HUMAN
FORM AND AMERICAN HISTORICAL THEMES.

*"I wanted comfort, beauty,
and warmth," says artist
Glenna Goodacre.*

It should not be a surprise that noted American sculptor Glenna Goodacre created her own bedroom in New Mexico. Her Santa Fe home was built to her own design. The western wall curves slightly, and the interesting ceiling features swoops of coved plaster between the 10-inch (22.5-cm) round wooden beams. "I wanted comfort, beauty, and warmth," she says, "and the focal point of the bedroom to be the views of the mountains and the city."

Goodacre has no problem thinking big: some of her most famous works are public sculptures, such as the Vietnam Women's Memorial in Washington D.C., the larger-than-life-size bronze of Ronald Reagan commissioned for his Presidential Library, and the monument to the Irish Potato Famine in Philadelphia. Her interest in Native American themes—seen in her design for the

Sacajawea or dollar coin for the U.S. Mint—is also evident in her bedroom decor.

She also designed the unusual headboard for her bed. It spans nearly the entire space of a wall, and incorporates bookcases, reading lamps, and even room to display a favorite painting.

The displays of art and family photographs reflect her eclectic lifestyle. But the bedroom really reflects an artist's sure touch in the selection and placement of objects, such as the antique fire screen she chose to front the fireplace built into a corner.

Amid these exotic details, smooth plaster walls, and generous window seating, Goodacre says she faced one mundane problem: "Where to put the TV. Problem solved: at the end of the bed, in an antique trunk. Press a button, the top rises, and voila! Every luxury!"

Above: This airy bedroom has an artful beamed ceiling and a view of Santa Fe.

Right: A painting of a classic nude.

This carved wooden table has intricately curved legs in a pattern echoed throughout the room.

The Design Details

BED AND BEDDING

"Originally I planned to have a centrally located bed," Goodacre said. "That idea was discarded when I realized I wanted to enlarge the sitting area by the windows. The wall that was left for the bed was too narrow to also accommodate bedside tables and lamps." The result is a "headboard-bookcase-cabinet."

WINDOW TREATMENTS

This home is high enough in the hills to dispense with window coverings; the room is open to light and overlooks a patio and sculpture garden. A wide, built-in ledge extends from the fireplace hearth to below the window (behind the armchairs). The ledge can be used for extra seating or display space.

WALL AND CEILING

The rough stucco commonly seen in "Southwestern" interiors has no place in this elegant home. Instead, the soothing look of smoothed plaster is used here as a more suitable backdrop for Goodacre's highly colored and ornately carved room furnishings.

The rounded wooden beams suggest the Spanish Colonial architecture used throughout the region. The ceiling is not a high one, but coving (curving) the plaster between the beams creates an illusion of height and extra space. The modern touch of a rotating ceiling fan is a necessary comfort in a hot desert climate.

Opposite: Bolsters and an abundance of pillows covered in paisley silks and cottons soften a tall custom-made headboard, a massive wooden construction with built-in bookcases and swing-arm reading lamps. The gold-painted frame for the painting is picked up by gold in the paisley bolsters and the pillows.

What Makes the Look: Choosing the Canvas for an Artful Selection

The eye of an artist is evident here in the mix-and-match of boldly colored fabrics for the bedspread, upholstered chairs, and area rug. But note the neutral colored wall-to-wall carpeting—it is a far better backdrop for the bright Navaho rug than a plain wood floor or clay-tiled floor would be.

Comfortable Retreats

Sometimes the most comfy bedroom is a family room—for couples to snuggle, for siblings and guests to share, and for children (and grand children) to be read to. Sometimes it is the calm center, the place to return for solitude and self-renewal. Family mementos, treasured photographs, and traditional design all add to the comfort of home.

Above: Ali MacGraw displays treasures from her travels.

Left: Philanthropist Nancy Davis' fairy tale enclave.

CHYNNA PHILLIPS

ACTOR, SINGER, AND FORMER *SEVENTEEN* COVER MODEL, CHYNNA PHILLIPS WAS BORN INTO A FAMILY OF ROCK STARS (MAMAS AND THE PAPAS) AND MARRIED INTO A FAMILY OF ACTORS (THE BALDWIN CLAN). SHE HAS TWO CHILDREN OF HER OWN.

Sentimental Journey

"[The] biggest problem was "getting everything in—it's a very small room," says interior designer Allan Warnick.

Married to actor William Baldwin and the mother of two children, singer Chynna Phillips lives mostly in New York and maintains this enchanting space in Santa Monica as guest quarters and West Coast refuge for herself and other family members.

The room is full of playfulness and attention to sentimental detail. A sleigh bed with musical notes painted on the headboard is the centerpiece of the bedroom. The notes are not random: designer Allan Warnick used the first few notes of Phillips' first number-one single. Warnick wanted this small bedroom to have an Alice-in-Wonderland feeling—Phillips's antique doll collection resides in the antique armoire.

Warnick softened the contemporary feel of the room by using English linens, lace, pale wall treatments, and unique hand-made and hand-painted furnishings. In fact, Warnick says his biggest problem was "getting everything in—it's a very small room."

But the room does not look small or feel cramped, despite all the things in it. The overall effect is comfortable and welcoming. This homey feeling traces directly to Warnick's attitude about interior design: "I simply select and design beautiful furniture and put it where it belongs in the room—then add flowers, lots of light, good smells, and the sound of the ocean if available."

Opposite: Allan Warnick designed the musical headboard and added the tulle shade to the antique lamp.

What Makes the Look:
Childhood Memories

Treasures collected when we are younger are no less precious over time. However, finding room for them until they can be given to the next generation can sometimes be a problem once we've grown up. Displaying such treasures in a guest bedroom, or one created in a pied-a-terre such as this one, personalizes the space and lends a homey touch.

Right: The vintage armoire, holding Chynna's doll collection, is a homey touch for this West Coast pied-a-terre.

Muted Harmony

ELEKTRA RECORDING ARTIST NATALIE COLE
CARVED OUT HER OWN NICHE IN THE WORLD OF
MUSIC WITH HER STYLISH AND "UNFORGET-
TABLE" INTERPRETATIONS OF THE JAZZ AND POP
CLASSICS ASSOCIATED WITH HER FATHER, THE
LATE NAT "KING" COLE.

Interior designer Lynn Palmer managed a major transformation by using a soft almond color for both walls and fabrics.

A sanctuary, a retreat—that is the basis of Lynn Palmer's bedroom design for singer Natalie Cole.

Some practical thinking helped, too. The previous owner of this sprawling California home had done it up as a French-style villa, with pink walls and carpeting that Cole did not like. Palmer managed a major transformation by using a soft almond color for both walls and fabrics. This subdued, one-dimensional color scheme gets its necessary sophistication, the designer notes, from "a subtle modulation of textures, with interiors that harmonize completely with the existing background." She completely redesigned

the unadorned, simple pink marble fireplace into a custom hand-carved mantel and chimneypiece.

Warmth also comes from the antiques and contemporary furniture that draw from the past, and gatherings of family photographs in gilt-and-silver frames. While Cole was on tour during the room's construction, says Palmer, "unbeknownst to her, I had gathered her most treasured photographs and placed them in gorgeous antique sterling silver frames. As she entered the room, she was so excited—saying it was just like the feeling she experiences Christmas morning, but even better!"

Soft almond color envelops a room and modernizes the concept of a canopy bed.

The Design Details

BED AND BEDDING

Palmer's tour de force is her modernization of a canopy bed: Instead of ruffles, both canopy and bed skirt are formal box pleats; the mitered corners of the cloth are set off with dressmaker-pleating detail. Gold braid on the trimly striped draperies makes the canopy snappy—and modern.

The upholstered bed was custom made for Palmer by CustomTouch for Interiors, a Los Angeles studio. The fabrics are from Scalamandré, and the wall-to-wall carpet is a deep-pile wool by Stark.

WINDOW TREATMENTS

Because the bed itself is elaborately draped, long draperies at the windows might have been too heavy for this light and airy space. So windows that were undistinguished architecturally got a facelift from Palmer's choice of a boxy, square valance and some matching pleated Roman shades, which complement the canopy of the bed.

What Makes the Look: On Beyond Beige

"Neutral" doesn't have to mean boring. The almond shade shown here in fabric and walls looks richer and warmer than ordinary beige or tan. Next time you are in a paint store, examine all the alternatives in the gold-to-brown spectrum. These can create more sophisticated walls than beiges with pinkish, peachy, or greenish tints.

Heroic
Proportions

NFL FOOTBALL STAR, SPORTSCASTER, AND
CHARITY SPOKESMAN BOOMER ESIASON AND
HIS SON, GUNNAR.

"[Boomer] likes big furniture with lots of comfort, styled on the masculine side," says designer Ivan Dolin.

Boomer Esiason is a big man. The six-foot-five (2 m) former NFL football star quarterback, sportscaster, and charity spokesman "likes big furniture with lots of comfort, styled on the masculine side," says designer Ivan Dolin. But the taste of Esiason's wife, Cheryl, "is very tailored and low key—so the mix is always interesting."

This is very much a bedroom for a couple that shares a preference for crisp, white linens and "always have had an important bed on a grand scale," according to Dolin. Here, a bed of vast proportions is the centerpiece for a collection of new and antique English-style furniture, made rugged for this Western home by the sage-green walls (both Esiasons'

favorite color) and an extra-large club chair covered in a Navajo-inspired fabric that matches the rug.

Esiason is not all football: he also runs the Boomer Esiason Foundation for Cystic Fibrosis, a charity he founded after his son, Gunnar, was diagnosed with the disease in 1994. Gunnar's presence is subtly noted in the design of this bedroom, which, for his sake, had to be designed to be as dust-free as possible. Among the very personal accessories are family photographs, a painting by family friend Elaine Patarini, a 1930's antique football helmet, and a green-and-white game ball given to Boomer for making 30,000 yards in his earlier career.

Opposite: The smooth ceramic fireplace extends to the 16-foot (5 m) ceiling. Robert Byrd, developer, provided the built-in cabinets of reclaimed pine.

This modern rendition of a George III bed
with carved mahogany posts borrows
a bit of pedigree from the eight-drawer
tallboy, a nineteenth-century antique.

A nineteenth-century "crotched mahogany" English chest is just tall enough to serve as a bedside table, one that is appropriate in scale to the large bed frame.

The Design Details

PALETTE
Sage green is the wall color, a fine complement to the dark woods of English and English-inspired furniture collected by designer and client.

FURNISHINGS
Dolin says his biggest challenge was "finding a bed big enough for Boomer that Cheryl could get up into!" The solution was a carved mahogany four-poster bed by Century, a contemporary manufacturer. Matching its bulk and its elegance is a nineteenth-century English style Highboy, mahogany with satinwood inlay. Artwork on the walls is a similar mix of contemporary paintings and collected landscapes in traditional oils and delicate watercolors.

WINDOW TREATMENTS AND FLOOR COVERINGS
Not shown here are light-blocking window shades, for daytime sleeping—a must to accommodate Boomer's broadcast and travel schedules. The faux zebra rug, from ABC Carpet in New York, comes in several sizes besides the "extra large" shown here.

SPECIAL ITEMS
The existing fireplace with its tall chimney, 11-foot (3.3 m)-high entrance doors and an adjacent bath with a 36-inch (91 cm) vanity sink score the right proportions "for someone who is a big guy, both on and off the field," says Dolin. But Cheryl Esiason loves the room as well.

To bring coziness to a room with 16-foot (5 m) ceilings, he honored Cheryl's request for worn finishes ("Cheryl hates glossy finishes") and made sure the bronze lamps and picture frames had a bit of patina—to make it seem as if the Esiasons had always lived among this furniture.

"The night of the final installation was their anniversary," Dolin recalls. "They walked in and called me at my hotel and said, 'It's great! We love it!'"

What Makes the Look: Period Woods

Furniture in the nineteenth-century English style known as George III appeared in Colonial American homes in the same era, and the weighty elegance of finely turned mahogany still matches well with more rustic furnishings in American homes.

To create a similar bedroom, look for antiques or reproductions in dark-toned woods that are enlivened with inlays or accentuate the wood grain. George III tables, chests, and tallboys are often found in "crotched mahogany," which has a flame-like grain. Sometimes these pieces show up in figured walnut, which has a burly grain.

Pay attention to scale and size. The tallboy shown here is more than a match for the giant-sized four-poster bed, but if the bed you have is smaller, use a smaller bureau as well. Note that the smaller bureau here is used as a bedside table.

Throw rugs placed under a bed can be proportioned to spill generously around the sides; smaller beds will look fine with small throw rugs placed beside them.

ALI MACGRAW
Simple Serenity

ALI MACGRAW STUDIED ART HISTORY AT WELLESLEY AND WORKED AS A PERSONAL ASSISTANT TO DIANA VREELAND AT *HARPER'S BAZAAR* BEFORE WINNING HEARTS AS AN ACTOR IN THE MOVIES *GOODBYE, COLUMBUS* AND *LOVE STORY*.

"I think the word 'designer' may be a bit much for what I did with this tiny house," says actor Ali MacGraw.

From the ashes of the disastrous Los Angeles fires of 1993 there rose, phoenix-like, a more meaningful bedroom for Ali MacGraw—in New Mexico. The actor and author had bought a tiny getaway house there before her Malibu home was destroyed. She made it into her permanent residence after the fire. The bedroom's design, she says, was dictated by its small size: "The queen-sized bed could only go in one way—looking out the window to the incredible mountains, which are called the Sangre de Cristos, when the late sunset bathes them in blood-red light."

What MacGraw clearly did bring to New Mexico was her style and a personal serenity that one might expect from a lifetime of yoga study. "I think the word 'designer' may be a bit much for what I did with this tiny house," says MacGraw. Beyond adding a bathroom, she made no architectural changes and over the years has added little in the way of new furniture. "I fell in love with an old French iron washstand, and I use it mainly for enormous bunches of flowers and as a place to put some of my treasures—bracelets, photographs, special books."

The small Shaker armoire had been in storage for nearly twenty years. The 1993 fire destroyed almost everything else she had possessed. But the flames spared MacGraw's collection of Tibetan and Rajasthani jewelry, some of her rugs, and a picture of her mother, drawn by her father, which she displays near photos of herself with her son, Josh, and of her beloved animals.

The pegboards are home to a constantly changing array of jewelry and textiles. "I guess I've always had a kind of nomadic mentality," says MacGraw. "With fewer possessions, there's the possibility, freedom, and desire to travel." Within the simple framework of her classic American furniture, the room has become a repository of memory and a refuge.

All of the decorations have a special meaning to her. She can tell you exactly when and where she found each piece, and tell you its history. While the display "may always be changing," says MacGraw, "there will probably always be a few familiar things which will speak to me about people and adventures and even fantasies which mean something to me—therefore, I will feel 'at home.'"

Opposite: Collected treasures above the vintage Adirondack chair include a hand-knit sweater (Kaffe Fassett, London); Native American silver and turquoise pawn jewelry; and a contemporary small deerskin medicine pouch, beaded in Indian style.

In serene whitewashed surroundings,
fabric, art, and jewelry dangle from a
simple Shaker pegboard. Lace-edged
pillows are piled on the bed, and fresh
wild flowers gathered from the grounds
are talismanic—they speak of travels,
as well as the comforts of home.

With its hand-rubbed adobe walls, brick flooring, bleached-wood ceiling, and simple country furniture, this bedroom might look austere without the personalized decorations of its owner. The creatively designed clothing and jewelry are not hidden away, but displayed and enjoyed when not being worn. Similar collections of hats, scarves, and jewelry can be mounted on walls with simple hooks and pegs, as seen here, to create a bedroom sanctuary full of happy memories.

The Design Details

PALETTE

There are many ways to work with the Santa Fe style of architecture and its ever-present vigas, but MacGraw's version is more "American country" in its serene purity of light tones. The ceiling beams are whitewashed, as are the rough-textured adobe walls. Bedding and lace curtains are finely textured feminine fabrics in pure white. The only terra cotta tones are in the brick flooring, which tops a radiant-heat system and is partially covered by Eurasian, not Native American, wool rugs.

FURNISHINGS AND FABRICS

Ali MacGraw's collection of classic American furniture reflects a lifetime of combing through antique stores in many states. The painted iron bed

(American) was found in Santa Monica; the complementary iron washstand (French), nineteenth-century wooden side table, and lamp made from a cast-iron final were discovered in Santa Fe. The nineteenth-century Shaker armoire, traditionally painted in deep green, dates to when she lived in New York City. The vintage Adirondack chair is from Richard Mulligan, in Los Angeles. The lace-edged bed linens are vintage Victorian, and like the sheer lace curtains, were purchased in London.

Above: Side table and lamp, made from a cast-iron finial, are finds from American Country, a shop in Santa Fe.

Left: Monoprint by Santa Fe artist Carol Anthony. The antique washstand is used to display fresh flowers and fabric treasures from Bali and Bangkok.

An Inside Edition

EMMY-AWARD WINNING BROADCASTER
DEBORAH NORVILLE IS AN ANCHOR,
PRODUCER, AND FIELD REPORTER
FOR THE SYNDICATED NEWS PROGRAM
INSIDE EDITION.

"They wanted the bedroom to be a sanctuary and retreat— something tranquil and soft, away from the hectic pace of New York City," says interior designer Sandra Nunnerley.

Television personality and newscaster Deborah Norville's New York City bedroom was designed around a lamp. Two, actually—a pair of terra cotta lamps that she and her husband, Karl Wellner, love. Designer Sandra Nunnerley used the lamps as the underlying theme for this room, giving the walls a special paint treatment that provides a warm inner glow.

"They wanted the bedroom to be a sanctuary and retreat—something tranquil and soft, away from the hectic pace of New York City," says Nunnerley. But the space had problems typical of those in Manhattan apartments. One window faces a side street, so the room design had to allow maximum light to come in but also had to block a rather ugly view. Another window faces a park, and Norville wanted a window seat from which to look out upon the calming greenery. The bedroom is small, could not be expanded, and had to contain functional accessories

for a busy news producer—like a phone by the bed and a reading light.

Nunnerley handled Norville's requirements with taupe and cream walls, brushed soft satin sheer curtains, and, of course, an amply pillowed window seat. The dappled, soft-mushroom wall treatment painted by Colorado artist Michael Battaglia has a light gloss, "to give a satiny, textural feeling," says Nunnerley.

The light and airy furniture is traditional, also by request. "Karl Wellner is Swedish, and Ms. Norville also has Swedish roots," says Nunnerley. The tall white chest is a necessity, given the smallness of the room, and Nunnerley used dressmaker details to add a tidy look to the sweetly feminine bedspread. "I took details from fashion," says Nunnerley. "For instance, I put flat bows on the bedspread, and on the matching headboard. The idea came to me from an evening dress."

What Makes the Look: Adding Inner Light

The inspired wall treatment uses several different shades and textures of semi-gloss paint in creams, taupe-mushroom, and a soft terra cotta. A similar, softly reflective effect might be created by using small sponges to apply paint, repeating colors in a widening, more-or-less circular pattern from a starting point at the top of each wall.

Urban windows get the soft treatment with sheer brushed satin. A balloon shade decorates the window seat, while a more casual drape is used for a side window.

Inner light effects for a city bedroom include textured, reflective walls, sheer curtains, and mirrors. Terra cotta lamps and Old Master drawings (red ochre *sanguines*) above the bed were collected by the owners.

Country
Meadow

THE FOUNDER OF THE NANCY DAVIS FOUNDATION FOR MULTIPLE SCLEROSIS IS AN INSPIRATION TO THE ACTORS AND ATHLETES WHO JOIN HER EACH YEAR FOR CELEBRITY FUNDRAISERS AND THE "THE RACE TO ERASE MS."

"Fanciful accents, collectible treasures, soft colors, and pretty fabrics abound. These are the things she loves," says interior designer Lynn Palmer.

A simple square room becomes "a sun-filled summer's fantasy, awash in blue pastel," in Lynn Palmer's design of a guest bedroom suite for philanthropist Nancy Davis, who, to date, has raised more than $15 million through the Nancy Davis Foundation for Multiple Sclerosis.

"Memorable rooms, like memorable people, have special personalities," says Palmer. "The lovely, tranquil and dreamy atmosphere of this bedroom truly reflects Nancy Davis' warm, intimate, kind nature. Fanciful accents, collectible treasures, soft colors, and pretty fabrics abound. These are the things she loves, for they radiate such beauty."

The room was a simple square with few windows and little natural light. Now, several coats of soft blue paint illuminate the walls. A custom floral print on neutral carpet lightens the interior, and French doors have been installed to fill the room with light and warmth. "Lightening the color scheme and keeping the backgrounds simple," says Palmer, "dramatically transformed this simple square room into a slightly larger, more comfortable, cozy place."

The hand-painted bed itself is more than cozy. Palmer calls it "magical, soft, and enveloping, adorned with custom white and blue Italian linens—a marvelous retreat." It is also the natural focus of the room—making the room's function clear, while enveloping its occupant in charm and beauty.

The Design Details

FURNISHINGS
Painted furniture has a long history in European decor; the style shown here is sometimes referred to as "Country Swedish." Bed, bureau, dining set, foyer table, and step stool are custom and available from the Lynn Palmer Collection.

FLOOR COVERINGS
The floral pattern was created by the designer and rendered as a custom broadloom for Nancy Davis by Stark. The kitchen area is polished pine.

SPECIAL ITEMS
Adding a small dining area to the bedroom suite—complete with fresh flowers and heart-patterned earthenware—lets visitors know their privacy is cherished as much as their company.

With its pale blue walls, trimmed fluffy bedding, and floral-strewn carpeting, this playful design for a guest room can be adapted for a baby's room, or to please a daughter.

What Makes the Look: A Carpet that Connects
Try imagining this guest room suite without its posy-strewn carpeting, which extends to the small foyer and dining nook. Palmer designed the carpet's pattern of scattered flowers, working with the color scheme picked out by Davis for the painted furniture. The combination is an appealing one for a guest bedroom, and would also be appropriate for a child's bedroom that includes a play area. Despite the neutral background, the carpeting has a low pile for easier maintenance.

FROM JOANNA'S JOURNAL
Floral carpeting creates a joyful mood that can't be matched by plain or geometric designs. A different route to this country look might be to find floral wall-to-wall carpeting first, then hand-paint the bedroom furniture to match the design.

PAULA ABDUL

Rose-Colored Calm

LOS ANGELES NATIVE PAULA ABDUL EARNED HER POP STRIPES AS A CHOREOGRAPHER FOR MUSIC VIDEOS, THEN RELEASED THREE OF HER OWN ALBUMS, INCLUDING THE PLATINUM-SELLING *SPELLBOUND*.

"She wanted this fairly small bedroom to be a retreat from her busy world," says interior designer Gary Gibson.

Gary Gibson had only four weeks to decorate an entire Los Angeles home for singer, actor, and dancer Paula Abdul. He had to work at a frenetic pace to create a bedroom that would be a safe, soothing, relaxing hideaway from the world. Abdul "wanted the feeling of a little European bed and breakfast," says Gibson. "She wanted this fairly small bedroom to be a retreat from her busy world—a place where she could come to feel instantly relaxed."

The designer took this cue to enlarge and completely revamp the master bathroom as a very private boudoir. "I basically had to start with a clean slate. The adjacent bathroom was all black and white with black fixtures. We had to gut the whole thing, switching to a white-and-pale-pink tile." To create the effect of a larger bedroom suite, all the walls and ceilings are colors that gently evoke the glowing facets of rose quartz, in a random pattern that makes the bathroom "melt" into the bedroom space.

He also added a phone to the vanity sink, a steam head to the sunken bathtub, and a swivel chair painted to match the walls.

Gibson's favorite memory of the project is of Abdul's first entrance into the finished bedroom suite: "It was evening, the lights were set, candles lit, flowers everywhere, fireplace going. When she entered, tears of joy appeared. I was delighted. It's the best feeling you can achieve with a client."

Spot lighting with softly
frosted bulb fixtures add to
the cozy feeling of a softly
draped bed.

A modest collection of twentieth-century art, such as the tiny bronze dancer and some examples of Lalique glass, can be glimpsed on the vitrine shelves.

The Design Details

PALETTE
Lavender, dusty rose, and gray with accents of pale pink and eggplant. Combinations of these colors were sponged onto the walls and the ceiling. Says Gibson: "We wanted it to feel cozy and almost cave-like."

THE BED AND BEDDING
Gibson, who has his own line of modern furniture, designed the bed and then covered it simply with soft pink linens and textured tab curtains in a shade of dusty rose.

OTHER FURNISHINGS
The cone-shaped chair in the bathroom is a Gibson design. Artworks, memorabilia, and family photos were gathered on two demi-lune bedside tables and in a lighted vitrine built into one of the bedroom walls.

Gibson has worked with Abdul on other projects, but he says, "To this day, this is still one of her favorite rooms."

What Makes the Look: Soft Color Tones

Paula Abdul's bedroom suite is a softly swirled mixture of lavender, rose, and pale pink— like the many shades one finds in crystalline rose quartz. It looks feminine but not old fashioned, thanks to Gibson's modern furniture and the reflected surfaces of glazed bathroom floor tiles and quite a bit of glass shelving. This "crystal" motif was used in both the bedroom (in the vitrine) and in the bathroom (vanity table).

Small touches help build the soft mood. Fresh flowers in glass vases, scented candles, and a pile of plush towels in the bathroom are everyday luxuries that soothe in an instant.

Some big, modern touches also lend their ease. Is there any woman who wouldn't love to have a telephone and a chair to chat in, in a room that also holds a large and luxurious steam bath?

Feminine pink tiles, a wall-sized mirror, and a cone-shaped swivel chair repeat and reflect the color tones found throughout this tiny bedroom suite.

Exotic Retreats

Thoughtful travelers pour the experiences of their travels into bedrooms that welcome them home to peaceful rest or artistic contemplation. Meaningful spaces become architectural expressions of a spiritual quest; memories and personal talismans are interpreted in unusual fabrics, patterns, and objects that seem to speak a different emotional language.

Above: Wesley Snipes' zen-like setup.

Opposite: Lotus flowers bring an Eastern influence to designer Renzo Rosso's home.

Soul of the Souk

ACTOR, INTERNATIONAL SUPERMODEL, AND VICTORIA'S SECRET CATALOG STAR TYRA BANKS BROUGHT A DISTINCTIVELY AFRICAN FLAVOR TO HER LOS ANGELES RETREAT.

"Doing Tyra's bedroom gave me the opportunity to fully explore an exotic locale without leaving Los Angeles," says interior designer Kevin Brian Burns. "As a production designer for films, I've done mostly urban environments. Now, I'll be ready when Hollywood decides to do a sequel to Casablanca.*"*

Fashion supermodel Tyra Banks brought home to Los Angeles more than souvenirs from her photo shoots in Morocco. She also brought home a desire for a Moroccan-style bedroom.

Keith Brian Burns, a production designer for films as well as an interior designer, took to the project immediately, creating a warm, exotic bedroom that incorporates Banks's collection of silver and brass accessories with detailed engravings, her interest in furniture from other cultures, a love of flowers and, says Burns, "the Zen philosophy of keeping low to the ground, keeping life simple while working in the fast-paced world of fashion."

This is a room for relaxing, with a low platform bed on the floor and plenty of pillows to recline and lounge upon. The headboard is an antique wool carpet, a nod to the fact that in the Old World, fine rugs are not just floor decor, but also used to soften seating or may serve as wall or window coverings. The diagonal placement of a large Berber rug, at a forty-degree angle to the bed itself, makes the room seem more spacious, as do the glass double doors that lead to a small courtyard garden. The tiled table, potted tropical trees, and ochre-painted walls continue the romantic feeling of a desert oasis—a private *casbah.*

"Communicating with Banks during construction was a challenge," says Burns. "She was modeling in Paris, nine hours later than Los Angeles, so the project survived on Federal Express, faxes, and telephone calls at odd hours to confirm furniture and furnishings."

The room is as authentic as planned. Banks brought home rugs that "smelled as if she just got them off the camel," says Burns, "and when the Santa Ana winds pass through Los Angeles, there is still a slight but distinct fragrance."

Bedroom as bazaar: Floor pillows and a low bed frame coupled with the ochred-pink walls that are traditional to Moroccan interiors help transform Tyra's Mediterranean-style California villa into an exotic bohemian retreat.

The Design Details

PALETTE

According to Burns, the deep ochre red used on the walls in Tyra's bedroom is authentic to Moroccan interiors. It is the same hue of the local bricks used to build the *medinas* and mosques of Marrakesh. The effect is a shady room with a cozy glow.

Strong, bright colors such as these may be favored in Marrakesh, yet are just as appropriate to decorate a home like this, one situated in the harsh, Mediterranean-like sun of Los Angeles. If your climate is more temperate, adjust to lighting conditions and look for fabrics and floor coverings in more subdued red or yellow tones (cinnamon, saffron, mustard, terra cotta) with accents of deep blue and white.

FURNISHINGS

Moroccan handicrafts include weaving, woodcarving, tilework, and fine metalwork. The most common wood used is cedar, which is carved, incised, or decorated with wood or tile inlay. Look for cutouts in an ogee shape or notched fretwork. These details appear as well in filigree metal lamps and lanterns that may be used for candles or fitted for electric bulbs.

Hammered metal tables, often round or octagonal, are another signature in Moroccan interiors (see "Mixing Metals"), as are furnishings decorated with brightly colored ceramic tiles. The tile-topped round table in the palm-decorated courtyard garden, seen just beyond the double glass doors, is a contemporary rendering of the intricate Moroccan tilework known as zillij. What is distinctive is the tiles are sealed but not glazed, so surfaces will have a rough, matte finish instead of the polished high gloss found in European tile.

Plain wooden furniture can be adapted for a Moroccan bedroom by tiling surfaces—or by simply topping a bedside table with a hammered, etched, and patinated metal tray. Plain furniture may also be painted with Arabic designs—as was done in the storage chest to the left of the window. Drawer pulls and other furniture hardware can be switched to dull brass or black iron.

WINDOW TREATMENTS

Smaller windows are dressed with sheer cotton muslin, with the extra-large tassels in golden silk leaving no doubt that this intimate mood is an exotic one. The glass doors leading to Tyra's courtyard garden were left bare to let in light and air. For this to work, door frames should be sanded before painting and hardware must have a finished look.

FLOORING AND FLOOR COVERINGS

Tyra's own collection of authentic Moroccan rugs illustrate the zigzags, diamond shapes, and double and triple borders that are all hallmarks of Berber designs. Both knotted ("oriental") and flat-weave (kilim) rugs can do the most to establish a Moroccan theme in a bedroom: smaller rugs can also be used to drape an armchair or, as here, to make a headboard.

If you can't get to the *souk* yourself, carpet importers and some major department stores (including Bloomingdale's, Macy's, and Conran's) sell contemporary Berber rugs, which are still woven in small villages throughout Northern Africa. A few reproductions in wool (or a soft polypropylene) from American or Belgian looms can help stretch the budget if you want to scatter an assortment of large and small rugs as shown.

What Makes the Look: Mixing Metals

Tyra's collection of silver, tin, and brass accessories all have a similar, burnished patina that gives them the charm of precious antiques.

To create a similar bedroom in Moroccan style, look for antiqued metal accessories, including rustic iron lanterns, hammered brass tables, and engraved metal incense burners at Asian import stores.

Silver objects in Tyra's room have a mellow glow. Unlike the sterling in your flatware drawer, engraved silver accessories should never be polished to a bright glare. Instead, allow the silver to oxidize naturally.

Surround antiqued metal objects with softer materials in subdued golds and grays. Earth-colored pottery and Indonesian wood tables, along with tasseled pillows and the coverlet, in burnished spice tones, make Tyra's bedroom cozy, not cold.

HISTORICAL NOTE

The particular shade of blue often seen in Moroccan design–picked out here in metalwork accessories and the deep blue goblets on the garden table— is typically painted on the front doors in Morocco for an old superstition holds that this color helps repel evil spirits. In Europe, designers call this deep azure "Majorelle blue," after Jacques Majorelle, a French artist who lived and worked in Marrakesh in the 1920s and 1930s.

Above: An embroidered and tasseled tablemat echoes the spice tones of Tyra's Kilim rugs.

Left: In Tyra's patio garden, a Moroccan contemporary table stands in for the blue-tiled courtyard fountains that are ubiquitous in Marrakesh.

Oriental Splendor

Dominating the room is an 1820 Anglo-Chinese bed frame, with an intricate gold design and crown-like decorations.

"We did things to the apartment that you usually do to a house," says New York designer Kenneth Alpert, speaking of the New York City interiors he created for actor Mary Tyler Moore. In the master bedroom, shown here, he created richly textured fabric walls and sculptural moldings at ceiling level to provide a strong and permanent backdrop for Moore's ethereal collection of lacquered and carved Chinese and European furniture.

Dominating the room is an 1820 Anglo-Chinese bed frame, with an intricate gold design and crown-like decorations. Gold leaf also distinguishes the French and English Regency desk, tables, and chairs.

Look closer and you'll see that this delicate oriental fantasy has its prac-tical side. Moore's apartment, which she shares with her husband, Dr. Robert Levine, is also a home to freely running pets, and Alpert's crafty use of fabrics acknowledges their presence without disarming the delicacy of the furniture. The bed-cover, for example, is not a fine silk but a sturdy cotton-linen blend, and the bed skirt is a simpler tailored fabric resistant to paw-marks. Silk damask was reserved for the chairs and some matching decorative pillows for the bed, and can be changed whenever Moore (or her dogs) tire of the gold-and-green color scheme.

The result is a bedroom that is comfortable as well as elegant.

Opposite: An 1820 English bed in a Chinese design is picked out with gold-leaf accents. Swing-arm lamps and a plain fabric bed skirt hint at the owner's practical streak.

The Design Details

PALETTE
Pale gold and cream, with gold accents on the furniture and wall decor. This is a neutral backdrop for an ever-changing display of contemporary art; Both Moore and her husband Levine collect paintings and sculpture as well as antiques. Shown on the left wall (see page 65): *The Open Door*, an oil painting by Henry John Stock (American, 1921).

WALL TREATMENT AND ROOM FABRICS
Wall and drapery fabrics are in a gold brocade from Lee Jofa. Just below the ceilings, the fabric has been accordion-pleated—a useful method to cover the vents of a central heating system. The pet-resistant bed fabric is from J. Robert Scott, and the low-pile rug by Edward Fields. The striped silk damask on the chairs and padded bench is tightly woven for long wear and can be Scotchguarded if needed.

FURNISHINGS
The 1820 Anglo-Chinese four-poster bed was discovered at Kentshire Galleries in downtown New York. A working desk in the bedroom is English Regency, with black ebony legs, brass inlays, and chunky brass claw feet. Elsewhere in the apartment, coromandel tables and Chinese import cabinets also have gold inlay.

Opposite: English Regency bedroom desk, with black ebony legs and brass inlays. Lamp, frames, and the blond storage unit behind the desk chair are contemporary.

What Makes the Look: Oriental, Expressed

Mary Tyler Moore's bedroom is a neutral stage setting for one high-impact piece of furniture: the Asian-inspired bed. Boosting the elegance level in your own home, you don't necessarily need to choose a bed. A beautiful Chinese cabinet, preferably a real antique, tall and inlaid with gold or mother-of-pearl, can cast the same delicate and romantic spell. A Korean wooden chest or large Japanese lacquered screen will work also. You can get an oriental effect in a very small bedroom with a single, significant and tall jar of elaborate export porcelain.

Choose a neutral wall treatment to set off the signature item, and match the inlay if you can. For example, a mother-of-pearl inlay suggests a milky blue or silvery gray for the walls. Brass and gold fittings can settle into backdrops of gold or beige. The rustic ironwork that binds Korean furniture can take deeper colors such as blue or green.

Instead of hanging fabric, sponge-paint the walls to create a similar feeling of soft texture. Camouflage ducts, heating pipes, and vents with the same paint.

FROM JOANNA'S JOURNAL
Use silk fabrics where they can be accented, and stick to easy-care linens for comforter covers, bedding, and curtains. You don't need much yardage for pillows or to make fabric shades for bedside lamps.

WESLEY SNIPES
Peaceful Pan-Pacific

ACTOR WESLEY SNIPES HAS APPEARED IN OVER THIRTY ACTION-ADVENTURE FILMS, FROM SCIENCE FICTION THRILLERS (*BLADE, BLADE II*) TO COMEDIES (*WHITE MEN CAN'T JUMP, MONEY TRAIN*) AND POLITICALLY INSPIRED DRAMAS (*UNDISPUTED, ONE NIGHT STAND*).

Architect and designer Jack Travis interpreted "the sincere spiritual essence" of his client with space, form, and large-scale shapes.

Architect and designer Jack Travis set himself a tall order in designing this Los Angeles bedroom for actor Wesley Snipes. The star of such international films as *Blade* and *Undisputed* wanted a retreat from the pressures of frequent travel, one that would merge a black cultural expression with a Los Angeles atmosphere, and that took into account the stunning views of a nearby beach.

"I wanted to infuse a *strong* sense of Afri-culturalism into a well-designed Western cultural envelope," says Travis. "Most times, African and/or black art can make the reference." But Snipes was also drawn to the clean lines of Asian interiors. So, Travis interpreted "the sincere spiritual essence" of his client with space, form, and large scale shapes that achieve a Zen-like simplicity, but owe their rhythm and structure to Afro-centric roots.

According to Travis, the low platform bed represents aesthetically—not literally—"what one finds in the grass and mud huts of West Africa."

He also had to be aware of Los Angeles realities. "The installation of the three large mirrors was a point of concern due to earthquake potential," says Travis. Snipes was reassured when Travis told him the mirrors would withstand any earthquake because he had "designed the bed area for the forces of a young male celebrity living in Hollywood!"

Travis' sense of humor about this residential project coexists with his seriousness of purpose: "The relationship of place of rest to floor is representative of the traditional African's relationship to Mother Earth. Here the floor is raised, celebrated in a sense, to receive the bed—the place of rest and peace."

Above: The expansive and soaring yet serene mood of this bedroom should come as no surprise to those who have followed architect Jack Travis in his career. Travis himself describes Snipes' building, a three-story townhouse, as "Neo-Corbusian Ocean Liner."

Left: A stylized African portrait gets a wall to itself in the bedroom's open foyer.

Stylish storage and the built-in
media cabinet were designed by
Redwing & Chambers.

The Design Details

PALETTE
Bedroom windows overlook a broad stretch of Pacific beach. Cool white was used for the walls as well as the carpeting.

FURNISHINGS
The platform bed is angled away from the windows and the mirrors, a feng shui touch that also complements the bed platform's capacity for relaxing at length at any angle. A circular mirror in the dressing area is a feng shui detail meant to channel light and energy around the room.

LIGHTING
Recessed lighting creates pools of illumination in the room after dark. A series of track lights along the back wall have fixtures that can be angled either towards the mirrors or away from their reflective surfaces. This can create different types of mood lighting in different areas of the bedroom.

What Makes the Look:
Balance on a Big Scale

Steps up to the platform give the room additional dimension. The broad expanse of carpeting, which sweeps up the steps, unifies the room and blurs the bed's boundaries.

The platform itself is angled at 45 degrees, veering away from a bank of windows to look towards an entertainment center built into a far wall. Entering the room, the effect may at first be slightly disorienting—but it offers a choice of walking directly towards the windows or mounting the low steps to recline and enjoy the view from a different, higher angle.

The three giant mirrors are essential, for they supply an architectural counterbalance to the big windows of this room and draw the eye upwards from the low-platform bed.

Clean white walls seem to demand large art, but scale and balance are still critical. "The challenge in art placement is to create the correct scale in relationship to the furnishings," says Travis, "which in this case were low to the floor." Where possible, large pieces were balanced by placing them across from a tall cabinet or by the strategic placement of a tall potted plant.

Siren Song

GRAMMY-WINNING SINGER, OSCAR-WINNING ACTOR, AND TELEVISION STAR CHER HAS NEVER BEEN AFRAID TO TAKE EVEN HER BEDROOM INTERIORS INTO NEW AND PASSIONATE DIRECTIONS.

"Cher's open-minded approach has allowed us to be experimental..." says designer Ron Wilson.

Sensuous and seductive, exotic yet familiar—this is the Los Angles bedroom of Cher. Beverly Hills designer Ron Wilson, who has created nineteen different residential projects for the movie star and singer, including bedrooms in several styles, employed his own appreciation of rich, neutral colors into the design direction of this master suite.

Fans of this vibrant stage and screen performer know Cher is always on the cutting edge of fashion and personal style. This incarnation finds her well grounded, as reflected by the stone platform for the iron four-poster bed, with its matching stone tables on either side.

Cher is "a discerning celebrity," says Wilson, and one with a love for "voluptuous upholstered furniture." As designer, Wilson is master of many styles and interior design themes, which helps, no doubt, in keeping pace with a client who is herself a master of style and self-change. "Cher's open-minded approach," he says, "has allowed us to be experimental during the twenty-plus years we have worked together."

7 2 BEDROOM RETREATS

Strong elements in this master suite include a stone platform for the iron bedstead and oversized furniture in rich black. Windows behind the banquette have Moroccan grillwork, and overlook a glass-ceilinged atrium.

The Design Details

BEDDING AND OTHER FABRICS

Totemic images of snakes have often appeared in Cher's bedroom furnishings, and here they are represented on the iron bed by bronze cobra ties. Fabric that surrounds the bed is a hand-woven Fortuny material, and the upholstered furniture is covered in a woven black-and-gold chenille from David Crowder.

What Makes the Look: Making the Change

Stylish people never shrink away from taking a new direction, either in life or in their home decor. Like snakes shedding their skin, a switch to innovative materials—in this case stone and black chenille seating—is always a liberating experience.

RENZO ROSSO IS THE OWNER/ FOUNDER OF DIESEL S.P.A., AN ITALIAN-BASED APPAREL AND FASHION COMPANY WHOSE FLAGSHIP LABEL IS DIESEL JEANS.

RENZO ROSSO

The Deep Blue

"The hardest thing was trying to convince the structural engineer that I was really serious about the fish tank," says designer Magnus Ehrland.

Opposite: Bedroom as chapel: The serenity of a seaside chapel is articulated through church-like leaded stained glass window treatments, and flooring of well-trod, 100-year-old oak planking. The sapphire blue tint of the fish tank wall brings the ocean closer.

Everything is visually striking in the Miami bedroom designed by Magnus Ehrland for Renzo Rosso, founder and owner of Diesel Jeans and Workwear. A fish tank, looming impossibly from inside the wall between the bedroom and the living room, was Ehrland's response to Rosso's desire for windows between the rooms, so that he could see the ocean while lying in bed. The bed is circular, and so is the fish tank.

"I thought windows would be an atmosphere killer," says Ehrland. Rosso uses this apartment to relax between trips to his North American stores and his factories in Europe, so the designer knew the architecture should be restful and serene. "Having the ocean view was very important to him. One day something went 'click' and I came up with the big round fish tank."

Other items are equally striking, such as the leaded stained glass windows behind the bed. On closer inspection one can see the window design incorporates the "RR55" trademark (for Renzo Rosso, born in 1955), which appears throughout his jeans and clothing line.

"One day in the beginning of the construction, Renzo asked me—like a kid asking for candy--'Please, Magnus, you think it's possible to put RR55 somewhere in the apartment?'" Ehrland recalls. "I said, 'Of course, just tell me if you want it big and shouting, or small and discreet, so you don't really notice it unless you are looking for it, or have a good eye for details.'"

In the end, a great many talismans and touchstones—such as Rosso's birthstone color, a rich sapphire—were incorporated into the room's design, Ehrland says. Glass nuggets of a deep sapphire blue center each window. Their church-like calm derives from a cross image so stylized it is barely perceptible, though hinted at through a grouping of ecclesiastical candlesticks on the headboard.

The Design Details

THE FISH TANK WALL

"The hardest thing was trying to convince the construction people and structural engineer that I was really serious about it," says Ehrland. To adjust for the weight of the heavy glass panels, the size had to be modified from a seven-foot (2.1 m) diameter to a five-foot (1.5 m) diameter, and additional support beams were required beneath the apartment's flooring—from the fourth floor down to ground level.

On the bedroom side of the wall, the fish tank has no frame, just a deep reveal that is painted sapphire blue. On the living room side, the wall surround is copper metal. "I got all these skeptical questions," Ehrland says. "How you gonna feed them? How will you change the water? Together with a fish tank specialist, we came up with good solutions that did not affect the design. I think it really adds a lot of character to the room."

FURNISHINGS

The *brio* of a Miami vacation home is well expressed in eclectic twentieth-century furniture, nearly all of it one-of-a-kind. The round bed dates with its curved Art Deco headboard hails from the 1930s; the blue plexiglass chairs are from the 1960s. Opposite the bed, a silver-metallic chest of drawers (circa 1960) is lit by a bronze lamp in the shape of a fish, with its original shade, made in 1953.

FLOORING AND ROOM FABRICS

The bedroom floor is recycled oak estimated to be 100 years old. The bedspread is a vintage chenille in ivory-white. "The panther in the chrome frame above the headboard is an old piece of boucle needlework, " says Ehrland. "His friend the leopard is not dangerous—or endangered."

BIRTHSTONE COLORS

In a system devised by medieval scholars, now perpetuated by Hallmark, each month of the year has a designated jewel. To wear the stone of your birth month brings luck; but only those born in October can wear opals safely, the legends say.

Month	Stone	Color
January	Garnet	Deep Red
February	Amethyst	Pale Violet
March	Aquamarine	Pale Blue
April	Diamond	Optic White
May	Emerald	Deep Green
June	Pearl	Pearly White
July	Ruby	Rich Red
August	Peridot	Pale Green
September	Sapphire	Deep Blue
October	Opal	Iridescent
November	Topaz	Deep Gold
December	Turquoise	Tropical Blue

What Makes the Look: Spiritual Colors, Letters, and Numbers

Renzo's bedroom is full of symbols that have a personal meaning for him, and he uses his birthstone color as a source of comfort. Birthstones are talismanic for many men and women who wear them for good luck. What are your birthstone colors? For many people, they are also a "favorite" color, often already included in bedroom color plans.

Monogrammed sheets have long represented personalized comfort in bedroom fabrics. The design of a monogram could also be stenciled upon a wall, or painted large upon a bedroom door. And keep in mind the capital letters in heavy wood, metal, or glass often sold as paperweights in stationery stores, to decorate a bookshelf or the top of a dressing table.

In casual or country style bedrooms, house numbers in polished brass, stainless steel, black ironwork, or sturdy wood from a hardware store may be arranged on a wall to signify important dates. Blue-and-white enamel house numbers look especially sweet in French country style bedrooms.

FROM JOANNA'S JOURNAL
A visit to a stained glass studio may convince you that a custom window, designed especially for you and including your own special symbols, could fit within your bedroom budget. Art schools can recommend nearby glass artists or have student workshops dedicated to glass art. The entire bedroom window need not be colored glass: consider hanging a stained glass panel in a frame that matches your window trim.

Above: The fish tank looks through into the apartment living room.

Right. The fish tank wall as viewed from the living room.

NATHALIE
HAMBRO

French Fantasy

"This room, like all others in the flat, is in constant evolution," says Nathalie Hambro.

The London-based designer Nathalie Hambro is well known for the highly architectural look of the handbags and accessories she creates, so perhaps it is no surprise that her living space is a vibrant mélange of fabrics, colors, and costume themes. What is surprising is how she's managed to make her small flat sleep three in sumptuous comfort.

Everything is multifunctional. In the living room, what looks like a long banquette are actually two narrow divan-beds pushed together. A cast-iron French daybed and a nineteenth-century chandelier allow the bedroom to serve as a private sitting room/library as well.

Like many typical London flats, there's not much light through the windows, so Hambro relied on fabric treatments to create a look she terms "cozy and atmospheric." The divans have "good mattresses," she points out, and are upholstered with a gold-striped cotton and with antique French damask curtain fabric.

The backing for the divans is a curving wooden screen, French, from the mid-nineteenth century (Napoleon III). The screen is called a *portiere*, says Hambro, and was commonly placed in front of doors to block drafts. This one has its original wool-and-silk fabric covering and was found in a flea market on the rue Jacob in Paris. Because the screen does not extend the entire length of the double banquette, heavy fabric panels were placed on either side. These provide a warm and comfortable backdrop for guests. "English walls can be cold," Hambro notes. A variety of antique fabrics, including Indian sari silks, cottons, and English Victorian beadwork were used for pillows.

"This room, like all others in the flat, is in constant evolution," says Hambro, who "rearranges" her things about every six months. "It is important not to get complacent with objects."

This small bedroom gains the grandeur of a sitting room with its collage art panel and formal touches that include a widestriped wallpaper, ormolu chandelier, and a daybed of elaborately scrolled cast iron.

A few heavy furniture elements, such as the curving wooden frame of the portiere screen, anchor an ethereal mix of glass and delicate fabric accessories. The orientalism of a later era in French decor marries well with this antique (French, mid-nineteenth century) and shows how such exotic touches add verve to traditional French furniture styles.

The Design Details

THE BEDS AND BEDDING

The heavily scrolled, cast-iron daybed comes from London's antique mecca, Portobello Road. The coverlets are striped cotton Burmese blankets. The divans in the sitting room are covered in an antique French damask, striped cotton, and sari silk.

OTHER FURNISHINGS

Whimsical touches include the cast-iron garden furniture and the top of a terra-cotta urn that was rescued from outdoor use and fitted with a glass round so it can serve as a table. As noted, the collection of accessories is ever-changing, reflecting Hambro's interests in antique textiles and intriguing wall art. A Piranesi panel in *grisaille* has pride of place in the bedroom, flanked by fabric tassels.

Opposite: Striped silk and cotton coverings for the divan beds, and an Ikat panel. "I love stripes," says Hambro.

What Makes the Look: Mixing Fabrics

At first it might seem that only a designer could manage the complicated mix of fabrics shown here. Look closer and you'll see there's a definite method employed. On the iron daybed and on the living room banquets, layers of striped fabric are placed geometrically, horizontal upon vertical and vice versa, resulting in a stabilizing "cross" effect.

Strong striped patterns on the walls—in the living room Ikat wall panels and in the wide green stripe of the bedroom wallpaper—reinforce the stability of the setting.

A few key pieces of heavy furniture also help to ground the more ethereal furnishings, such as the light silk and cotton pillows.

Modern Retreats

Elements of convenience, speed, and comfort are all taken into consideration in modern bedrooms and bedroom suites. High-energy interiors emphasize the joyful aspects of the journey with punchy colors, soaring architectural details, and luxury materials from around the world. These are the necessary ingredients for those who enjoy traveling in the fast lane.

Above: NBA star Derrick Coleman goes for bold.

Opposite: Minimalism is key in financier Marshall Coburn's NYC loft.

ANGEL SANCHEZ
Material

World

"My concept was to make this into a peaceful, dark, and self-sufficient hideaway." says interior designer Christopher Paul Coleman.

More than bold splashes of orange and strong lines draw your eye in Angel Sanchez's top-floor duplex in Caracas. The eclectic and exquisite materials chosen by designer Christopher Paul Coleman include gleaming white marble, tropical woods, rubberized cottons, and even animal furs. Like the couture fashions Sanchez is known for, every-thing is touchable, sleek, modern—and surprisingly comfortable.

The bedroom suite on the top floor has a style all its own. "It is a contrast from the rest of the house, an area closed off by double-height wenge wood doors," says Coleman. "It is a quiet space, very masculine and dark. He likes to read and relax here, watch videos of fashion shows. He's a very quiet person, and wanted space to contemplate creative thoughts."

Coleman, who is based in New York, has been a friend of Sanchez's for many years. He first arrived as the designer as the six-story house was being built. This allowed him to suggest some changes, for example the long skylight that spans the length of the attenuated dressing room/bathroom area that connects the bedroom to a separate small sitting area.

"My concept was to make this into a peaceful, dark, and self-sufficient hideaway," says Coleman. The "retreat" has a mini-library with a chaise longue, a Jacuzzi, and a bathroom with showers for two.

"You will notice there is very little pattern, except for the artworks and the long runner in the dressing room—so it is serene," says Coleman. The surfaces are clean and spare, while rich in texture. "The plan is very open, for easy maneu-verability."

Throughout, Coleman used some of the same materials Sanchez has used in his couture designs, such as the chaise longue, which is wrapped in a cowhide the designer had used to make handbags. The luxurious fox fur rug uses remnants of skins for fur coats.

Opposite: A wenge wall unit divides the bedroom from the dressing area.

The Design Details

THE BED AND BEDDING

To match the heavy paneled doors and the entertainment center opposite, Angel Sanchez designed his own platform bed with a wenge wood headboard. The two headboard panels are hinged so it can be "wrapped around" the side of the bed. The bed linens are "Granite Stripe," a high-weave cotton from the Calvin Klein Home Collection. The bed throw pillows are a charcoal-gray vinyl from Donna Karan, selected especially to complement the bedroom curtains.

WINDOW AND FLOOR

The full-length window is curtained with a high-tech polypropylene fabric used to make raincoats, and it has a soft rustle as it glides along a hospital track rod. The floor is tiled in polished white marble; the area rug is gray fox fur. The long wool runner is a custom design by Coleman, executed by Misha Carpet.

FURNISHINGS

American furniture from the 1950s in mahogany and chrome lends masculine appeal to the library-sitting area of the bedroom suite. The chaise longue is a vintage garden chair, upholstered in orange cowhide. And notice the tiny wire chair sculpture on the bedside table, a playful touch. The library desk was designed by Sanchez for an AIDS benefit; the companion cabinet (circa 1950) was purchased in Caracas.

The master bath and dressing area has a long skylight, so clothing fabrics can be viewed in natural light. The custom wool rug matches the wood and wall colors used throughout the master bedroom suite.

What Makes the Look: Playing with Surface Textures

Coleman has used a luxurious mix of materials—fox fur, metal wire mesh, and vinyl—that combine for an elegant, masculine look. All of his textural innovations can be easily adapted to create a sleek and modern bedroom.

An old fur coat you no longer wear can be salvaged, pieced, and bound around the edges to make a small throw rug for your bedroom floor. Elsewhere in the house, Coleman used flokati—traditional sheepskin fur rugs—another interesting option.

Wenge, a sustainably harvested tropical hardwood, is a modern choice if you're looking for a dark wood alternative to mahogany or teak.

Rubberized fabrics can be obtained from industrial suppliers, as can the metal rods.

Sanchez designed his own headboard, which can embrace the sleek platform bed. Rubberized vinyl curtains and a fox fur rug on polished marble floors are two stylish innovations by his designer, Christopher Paul Coleman.

Modern Traditions

BLUE NOTE RECORDS JAZZ VOCALIST CASSANDRA
WILSON HAS BEEN PRAISED FOR HER "DISTINC-
TIVE AND FLEXIBLE VOICE," AND FOUR ALBUMS
THAT RANGE FROM ACOUSTIC BLUES (*BLUE LIGHT
TILL DAWN*) TO A FREEFORM JAZZ TRIBUTE TO
MILES DAVIS (*TRAVELING MILES*).

"[Cassandra's bedroom] has bare-bones, pre-war detailing," says interior designer Tony Whitfield, "and it fills with a wonderful, soft, golden light at the end of a summer day."

New York City jazz vocalist Cassandra Wilson has a choice of two bedrooms, one for summer and one for winter. "Depending on the season, the light, and her mood," says designer Tony Whitfield, "her bedroom is either a Caribbean blue room looking southeast over Yankee Stadium, or a 10 by 12 foot (2.5 by 3.6 m) room facing northwest overlooking upper Manhattan." Wilson's available choices result from her occupancy of eleven rooms that were previously two apartments, but now are joined by a door between the two units.

Shown here is the small bedroom that faces northwest. "It has bare-bones, pre-war detailing," says Whitfield, "and it fills with a wonderful, soft golden light at the end of a summer day." Wilson said she wanted the space "to feel airy and relaxed, like there should be mosquito netting"—but it also had to accommodate a king-sized poster bed.

Both Wilson and Whitfield liked the idea of having "a room that feels like it's all bed." Once the bed was in place, very little was needed to furnish the room, but what is there complements the clean lines and elongated posts of the bed's cherry wood frame. Whitfield's own design for a cherry wood and steel armchair and bedside tables of steel and glass give this bedroom a modern rhythm, perfectly in tune with the Jazz Age architecture of its location in upper Manhattan's Washington Heights.

Opposite: Lightweight cotton fabrics, cool metal tables, and translucent Japanese paper shades keep the mood light in this summer bedroom.

The Design Details

BEDDING AND FABRICS

Whitfield says the modern lines of Wilson's cherry wood bed ruled out "lots of fabric and lace" but the result is still romantic with fine cotton bedding and a cool blue coverlet that's suitable to a summer bedroom.

FURNISHINGS

The brushed steel and glass bedside tables are medical tables made by Wyeth, which supplies them for hospitals. To complete the room, Whitfield added his "Dean LA" armchair, a modern design in cherry wood and steel. Wilson collected vintage photogravure and family portraits, an Asante stool, and African textiles. All of these elements reinforce the Jazz Age ambience of the room.

WINDOWS AND LIGHTING

Summer sunlight is welcomed in this bedroom, so the simple curtain treatment is cotton voile, looped on a rod. The wall-mounted bedside light fixtures were also designed by Tony Whitfield. Appropriately summery, they are two brushed steel sconces with large Japanese paper shades.

What Makes the Look: Modern Metal in a Bedroom

Industrial furniture, such as these metal surgery tables, often appear in living rooms, dining rooms, and kitchens in modern homes. Much of the appeal is that this furniture is low maintenance, highly functional, sturdily built, and well suited to people with active lives and busy schedules.

Tony Whitfield, who is a furniture designer as well as a room designer, has a new line of furniture that features sustainably harvested rainforest woods.

DERRICK
COLEMAN

Big and Bold

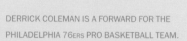

DERRICK COLEMAN IS A FORWARD FOR THE
PHILADELPHIA 76ERS PRO BASKETBALL TEAM.

"We had to basically gut the house and rebuild it," says interior designer Mark Morganroth. "We had to install eight-foot (2.4 m) doors throughout."

NBA basketball star Derrick Coleman wanted to live in the neighborhood where he grew up. So he bought the house next door to his boyhood home and brought in designer Mark Morganroth to adapt it to the life of the man he is today—an active athlete who is nearly seven feet tall.

"We had to basically gut the house and rebuild it," says Morganroth. "We had to install eight-foot (2.4 m) doors throughout—and even lower the floors to make the ceilings high enough so he feels in proportion to the size of the house." The house itself is small, so Morganroth created built-in cabinets for the master bedroom to create a spacious feeling. "It is a lot more work to tear down an interior of a house and rework the interior walls than build a new

house," the designer adds.

Coleman wanted a contemporary bedroom that could accommodate a large entertainment center, says Morganroth. This room looks big and bright, thanks to the floor-to-ceiling white wall units and sharp modern decor. The media wall features a 70-inch (1.8 m) TV that can disappear behind a remote-control-operated door.

The custom-made bed is a foot (30.5 cm) longer than normal, mandating as well some custom-made oversize sheets, blankets, and mattress. The bedspread is Morganroth's own design, executed in primary colors of Ultrasuede to match the artwork that became the main focal point of the room.

Right: The high energy of primary colors gains focus and restraint in an all-white room.

Below: The media wall features a 70-inch (1.8 m) television and surround-sound music system.

To minimize clutter, lamps were banished in favor of inset lighting, and built-ins were installed on two walls. This dressing area shows a cabinet layout scaled to Coleman, who is six-foot-ten (2 m) in socks.

What Makes the Look: Framing Bold Colors

The vibrant Ultrasuede bedspread features an abstract pattern of primary colors that has been "framed" in black, just like the painting above the bed. Designers, architects, and even landscapers have used this technique for decades, reining in the free play of bright colors within a "frame" that is typically a rectangle. Morganroth's use of a neutral background—walls, cabinets, and carpeting in bright white—also helps restrain the color splash.

Primary colors are always cheerful but they don't look child-like if you choose sophisticated fabrics. The designer's choice of Ultrasuede has great masculine appeal. Aniline-dyed leather or heavy silk might also work with this color plan.

Anchored Apartment

POPULAR TV NEWSCASTER BRYANT GUMBEL HOSTED NBC'S *TODAY* SHOW FOR 15 YEARS BEFORE MOVING TO CBS TO HOST ITS HARD-HITTING RIVAL, *THE EARLY SHOW*.

Interior designer John Barman created a bedroom for TV host Bryant Gumbel in which his work would be the unifying theme.

Most celebrities want bedrooms to which they can escape from extremely hectic schedules. Some want rooms where they can do at least a little work while relaxing away from the outside world. But Bryant Gumbel, former co-host of *The Early Show*, wanted John Barman to create a bedroom for him in which his work would be the unifying theme.

On the go as anchorman for a national television news show that airs at 7 AM five days a week, Gumbel "needed a home office that had a bed in it," says Barman, "a place to get away and be quiet or work. A private space."

It helps to remember that when Gumbel watches TV, he's not looking for entertainment. "He needs the TV for business," says Barman. "He also wanted a tall desk—this is the way he likes to work—and a place for his photos and books."

As usual in New York apartments, space became a significant design issue. "It is a small room," says Barman, but Gumbel "wanted it to be comfortable as well as convenient. "Barman's solution was a captain's bed, outfitted for organized storage, with an array of shelving and built-ins to make sure all the needs were met: "space for clothes, a place to pack, a place to nap, a place to watch TV, and space for a large, high desk."

Above: A captain's bed for a working bedroom is perfectly fitting for the home office of a TV "anchor."

Right: Framed magazine covers are cheery reminders of a distinguished journalism career that has gained Gumbel two Peabody Awards and the Edward R. Murrow Award.

MARSHALL COBURN

FINANCIER AND CO-FOUNDER OF THE RHYTHM ASSOCIATED MUSIC COMPANY, MARSHALL COBURN WAS ACTIVELY INVOLVED IN THE ARCHITECTURAL DESIGN OF HIS SOHO LOFT RENOVATION.

Downtown Style

Interior designer Beata Galdi "created the effect of transparent layers of space, with steel and glass modulating between the more intimate, cozy areas of the bedroom and the social, living spaces."

Where does a high-powered New Yorker like Marshall Coburn sleep? The bond trader and senior managing partner for Bear, Stearns and Co. makes his bed in a converted sewing factory—which he completely renovated with architectural and interior designer Beata Galdi.

Galdi credits Coburn himself with the idea of moving the bedroom to the mezzanine level of the loft, which is situated between two staircases, one that leads down to the first floor and another that leads up to a private roof. Because this bedroom must also serve as a passageway to the roof when Coburn entertains, the bedroom had to look highly organized and uncluttered as well.

Galdi's follow-through, she says, "created the effect of transparent layers of space, with steel and glass modulating between the more intimate, cozy areas of the bedroom and the social, living spaces." This turns the bedroom visually into a floating bridge that maximizes the openness of the loft interior.

Unexpectedly angled cabinets, in highly polished pear wood, and an asymmetrical location for the bed, carve the mezzanine level into a dynamic and sophisticated bedroom floor plan. Because the bedroom is only separated from the rest of the apartment by a low wall and a railing, the headboard is visible from the first floor. This became the room's dramatic focus, expressed by two planes of complementary materials. Its vertical plane is an angled sheet of perforated stainless steel; the horizontal is covered in soft fabric, which drops down on the right to meet the top of the bedside cabinets.

A modern loft bedroom that has the angles,
including storage cabinets with slanted drawers.
The bed frame is a custom design from Studio
Galdi. A staircase of glass and stainless steel
connects the mezzanine bedroom to a private
roof patio used for entertaining.

The Design Details

MATERIALS

The soft golden glow of polished pear wood and the sheen of stainless steel were used throughout the loft. Semi-opaque glass panels are the room dividers for a wardrobe and dressing area tucked away in the bathroom area behind a curving glass door, for example. "This picks up on the other glass elements throughout the apartment, such as the glass stairs to the roof," says Galdi, "and heightens the sense of transparency and lightness of the whole interior."

FURNISHINGS

Galdi designed custom furniture for Coburn, working closely with Brooklyn artisan Chris Perry. Low cabinets of pear wood create a continuous line along the back wall and along the side wall near the staircase. This line is unified by a slim, stainless steel base that runs along the bottom of all the cabinets.

On the right side, a series of "drunken cabinets" have drawers with fronts slanting on the diagonal. These are matched flush with the rest of the cabinets, a fanciful but understated expression of the angles used in the overall design.

FLOORING AND FLOOR COVERINGS

On the mezzanine level, the existing hardwood floor was retained, cleaned, and sanded to a smooth finish, then refined with a whitewash. The adjacent bathroom floor is a beautiful material, a high-quality slate from Norway, cut to fit the curving glass wall. Although a template was made to ensure that the unusually large slab would be cut to the right dimensions, the first slab did not fit precisely in the bathroom, says Galdi.

WINDOWS AND LIGHTING

Enormous floor-to-ceiling windows and a skylight fill the loft with natural light, so the designer used halogen lamps to achieve the correct balance between sunlight and artificial light throughout the rooms. Lighting such a large space required a series of lighting set ups, each one controlled with its own transformer.

For example, a row of tiny recessed halogen lights along the mezzanine creates what Galdi calls a "light shield" around the bedroom. It can be controlled with a dimmer switch. Soft, low-level bar lights (uplights) are recessed into the tops of the bedroom cabinetry.

The lighting in the bathroom is similar to that used elsewhere in the loft, and it illustrates a method than can be used successfully in other large-area interiors. This shows a cable wiring system with fixtures mounted directly from or between two low-voltage power-supply cables. The dangling lamps are soft halogen floods that can be aimed at selected surfaces and objects in a room, but because they are floods, not focused spotlights, the result is a wash of light, not a harsh illumination.

Big rooms don't need big lights:
Beata Galdi's lighting treatments for
her many loft clients often involve
small halogen floods that dangle
from installed low-voltage wires, as
seen in this spacious bath.
Recessed halogen "can" lights with
waterproof covers were installed
with the shower area.

What Makes the Look:
Hiding the High Tech

No man's loft would be complete without a communications
system and high-end audio and
video electronics for entertaining. What's exciting here is how
Galdi has incorporated a great
deal of high-tech within sexy and
elegant skins.

Steel cabinets on either side
of the bed serve as night tables,
which contain answering
machines and telephones hidden in pull-out shelves. There
is even a semi-circular tray that
swings out over the bed, and
bedside access to a remote
control for the loft's motorized
window shades.

Near the staircase, a stainless
steel cabinet with tiny perfora-
tions conceals a stereo
speaker, which is part of an
apartment-wide media system
that links the office/television
room on the first floor, the
kitchen, and a television
installed in the master bath.
A second steel cabinet in the
bedroom hides the HVAC.
Transformers for the lighting
system and other electronic
devices were hidden in the cabinets behind the storage areas
for books and clothes.

Backstage View

"Her personality is reflected in a sense of order and a complete understanding of simplicity—but still, it is luxurious," says designer Vicente Wolf.

How do you create an environment that is soothing, functional, and modern for someone who has a highly developed sense of order as well as a theatrical streak in her personal style? That was the challenge facing Vicente Wolf in designing this bedroom in a Greenwich Village penthouse for Shelley Washington, ballet mistress and co-production director for the Twyla Tharp Dance Company.

"The hardest thing was getting rid of all the ugly old stuff that was there previously," says Wolf. Out went the pink-painted floor and the Formica built-ins, leaving a room with wonderful rooftop views but very little storage space. The designer's solution is one that might gladden the heart of anyone who is a shoe collector or clotheshorse at heart.

A small adjacent room, which had previously been used as a child's bedroom, became Washington's new walk-in closet, a place where she could display as well as organize her collection of current and vintage designer clothes. A mirrored door now links this "backstage" dressing area to the bedroom.

With no bureaus or dressers to clutter the bedroom's living space, there was room for a sumptuous bed and a glamorous ruffled chaise, covered in Manuel Canovas wool. The result is a simplified room that, as Wolf says, suits Washington, who recently received a Bessie Award for her work in stage design: "Her personality is reflected in a sense of order and a complete understanding of simplicity—but still, it is luxurious."

Opposite: Banishing all dressing items to a walk-in closet meant that this penthouse bedroom could fit in a comfy chaise, as well as an unconventional, diagonal floor plan.

The Design Details

COLORS AND FABRICS

The monochromatic palette relies on textural fabrics. A sturdy, ridged sisal rug and pale linen window drapes and window shade are practical enough for a busy lifestyle. Frette linens on the bed and the comfy cashmere throw from Hermes on the wool-upholstered chaise are in similar shades of cream and tan.

FURNISHINGS

Propped-up mirrors and Washington's collection of vintage photographs in frames set the stage fittingly for a former dancer and award-winning stage designer. The orderliness of these squared objects is balanced by the soft, loose, and casual upholstery on the chaise and slipper chair. The matching slipper stool can be seen within the adjacent walk-in closet.

Properly organized, a dancer's collection of shoes gains the charm of a museum display, a theme abetted by the antique French mannequin and trim hatboxes.

What Makes the Look: The Clarity of a Closet

Without clothing clutter, bedding fabrics gain new emphasis and should be chosen for their textures as well as their ability to hold up over time. The comfortable cashmere throw is an investment piece, but this luxury material is also longwearing and durable, giving pleasure for decades with reasonable care.

If you're a clothes collector, consider sacrificing some bedroom space to make a walk-in closet. As seen here, a bedroom not cluttered with dressing furniture becomes more restful, and the new dressing area becomes a destination and second sanctuary.

If you can't add a full-size closet, consider replacing dressing tables and bureaus with built-in compartment shelving, floor to ceiling and fronted with plain wood doors painted to match the color of your bedroom walls.

To create an organized dressing room, build or select shelving units with compartment sizes that make sense. The narrow compartments shown here are perfect for storing shoes and handbags. (Not shown: pole racks on the opposite side for hanging garments). The assortment of sleek hatboxes matches the color scheme.

Natural Retreats

Gardens and favorite outdoor places inspire bedroom spaces that can be peaceful yet playful at the same time. The following outstanding designs don't mimic nature, but instead interpret the feelings evoked by natural life forms and natural light. By choice of wood, window, and wall treatments, the bedrooms that follow borrow from nature the sense of being enfolded in a leafy bower or waking up in the shelter of sturdy forest trees; modern lines and colors re-create the steady calm of a beach horizon in Montauk or the mysterious glow of a seashell found upon Malibu sands.

Above: Georgette Mosbacher's fantastic New York "Waterview."

Opposite: The summer bedroom of Stanley A. Weston.

MELODY BEATTIE

Coral Dreams

MELODY BEATTIE IS THE BEST-SELLING AUTHOR OF POPULAR SELF-HELP BOOKS, INCLUDING *CO-DEPENDENT NO MORE*, *BEYOND CO-DEPENDENCY*, *THE LANGUAGE OF LETTING GO*, *LESSONS OF LOVE*, AND *PLAYING IT BY HEART*.

Interior designer Antonia Hutt advised that the ever-present salt air causes fabric to disintegrate, and the strong sun would bleach them."We knew that in time, the colors would fade and produce a beautiful, washed out look."

The vast expanse of ocean outside a small 1920's beach cottage inspired the vibrant colors that decorate writer Melody Beattie's bedroom in Malibu, California. Designer Antonia Hutt wanted to bring in as much exotic and beautiful sea life as possible, and personally designed the large octopus-shaped mirror, a signature item for the room.

This bedroom was tiny, measuring only 11 by 13 feet (3.4 by 4 m)—not large enough for the author's previous king-size bed. Hutt not only found a new bed to scale, but also found tiny teak chests for bedside tables—then had to raise them to the right height for the bed. She decided to build platforms, which not only raised the chests but also provided additional storage space for the author's collection of books and magazines.

The room was painted a delicate pink, and the ceiling in a shade of very pale blue. Hutt knew that once the deep coral window shades were mounted, lighting shining through would add a mysterious glow, like the inside of a giant sea shell. The aura of tranquility this inspired seems perfectly in tune with Beattie,

the author of several popular self-help books.

According to Hutt, "Melody operates on a higher spiritual level than most people. So we wanted to create a space that is tranquil and serene, much like a meditation room." The strong, pure colors used by Huff are self-affirming in this context. Doors and woodwork were painted deep blue, suggesting the ocean behind them, while pure white bed linens of fine Egyptian cotton and the finely gauged mosquito netting lend a tropical touch.

Letting go—and letting the forces of nature take their toll on the natural fabrics—was also part of the plan. Because the house was close to the ocean, Hutt advised her client that the ever-present salt air causes fabric to disintegrate and the strong sun would bleach them as well. "We knew that in time, the colors would fade and produce a beautiful, washed out look," says Hutt. She did use "an industrial grade oil paint on the woodwork" to preserve the painted surfaces a bit longer, and changed the door and window hardware to solid brass, to slow down the corrosion caused by salt air.

This beachside bedroom features teak furniture, a wood that withstands the aging effects of salt air. The delicate mosquito netting came from Pier One Imports; the striped blanket is by Pendleton.

A collection of seashells is all the art this simple room requires.

The Design Details

FURNITURE AND FABRICS
The headboard is made of lavender-hued terrycloth; lavender cotton makes the bed skirt and toss pillows. The furniture in the bedroom and throughout the house is mostly Indonesian teak, a wood historically used for its ability to withstand the warping and aging effects of salty ocean spray.

SPECIAL ITEMS
The octopus image for the mirror is a design that Hutt had drawn frequently, even when she was a little girl. "Here was my chance to do my favorite design," says Hutt. "I just had to increase the scale!" The mirror was created by local artist Arnold Steele from broken tile and glass in shades of blue, aqua, and green. To evoke the ocean further, Steele mixed his tile grout with sand to give it the right color and a appropriate, slightly gritty texture. An assortment of exotic seashells on the bedside chests was repeated throughout the house.

"Along with the constant hum of the ocean," Hutt says fondly in retrospect, "This was a pleasure to do."

The mosaic tiled mirror and vibrant blue doors add some necessary definition to simple cottage architecture.

What Makes the Look: Playing the Shell Game

Seashell colors are always soothing in a bedroom. The dark coral color is used here sparingly, in the Roman shades and a bed pillow. (Used on the walls, a dark coral would make this small room look more like a cave than a seashell.) To achieve a similar glow on a pink-painted wall, choose coral fabric for your bedroom lampshades.

The deep pinks, blues, and purples seen here would fade over time, as would the colors of the Turkish kilim carpet. Try imaging a similar room in a vacation beach house with all these colors softened, the way beach glass appears in frosted blues and greens when it has been tumbled and polished by the ocean waves.

Seashells by themselves are a lively motif for bedroom decorations. Notable specimens of large size, such as the pointy conch shells, the broad, iridescent bowls of abalone, and the pearly carapace of the rare nautilus might be mounted and displayed like works of art. Look for these in the gift shops of natural history museums, or collect them when vacationing at seaside resorts.

STANLEY A. WESTON

Man of
All Seasons

STANLEY A. WESTON HELPED PIONEER THE TOY MERCHANDISING INDUSTRY IN THE EARLY 1960S WITH "ACTION FIGURES" SUCH AS G.I. JOE, AND REMAINS AN INNOVATOR IN TRADEMARK LICENSING AND MOTION PICTURE PRODUCTION.

Designer George Constant created a winter bedroom and a summer bedroom. Weston uses them both, depending on the season.

You might expect the country home of Stanley Weston, creator of the world-famous G.I. Joe action figure empire, to be filled with military memorabilia. But it turns out that Weston's eclectic tastes run more toward the Old West—a theme that was carried through two very different master bedrooms in the same house.

Designer George Constant created a winter bedroom and a summer bedroom. Weston uses them both, depending on the season. The winter bedroom is dark and rich, says Constant, because Weston "likes dark wood—rich colors. I worked very hard to make it sparkle a bit, with metals, high-intensity lighting, and color accents."

The horn settee—an authentic bit of the American West from the early twentieth century—complements the bold American Star quilt. Much like a pioneer's wagon might have been packed with furniture treasures that had city roots, Constant filled the bedrooms with "the quirky things I found for him, which got him quite excited." Among those

things are once-tall Chinese night stands, their bottoms cut off by Constant to create night tables, Italian side chairs from Naples, and the English painted-glass chessboards that decorate the wall above the headboard in the winter bedroom.

The summer bedroom is lighter, at the other end of the house and overlooking a swimming pool. The majestic four-poster bed was made of leftover timbers from the house: the heavy beams are the same used into frame and brace the bedroom ceiling. "I sketched a bed and the builder built it," says Constant. "It weighs about four million pounds."

This room's American West items include a Frederick Remington sculpture—one of eight owned by Weston—and small details such as the cow-shaped iron doorstop, painted black-and-white and perched on a night table. The eclectic mix includes a rare "League of Nations" quilt, hand-made American Adirondack, tables and chair, an old English ram's head, and scatter rugs in lavish oriental designs.

Left: The summer bedroom continues the interplay of heavy, rustic materials with refined, artistic accents. A Navaho rug, Frederick Remington bronze, and cheery bouquet of sunflowers show how to civilize a Western-style interior.

Below: In the winter bedroom, the geometric pattern of an American Star quilt plays off the reverse-glass paintings, which are antique chessboards from England. This refined geometry extends to the bed frame, an elegant foil to the rustic planking walls.

What Makes the Look:
Civilizing the Old West

Stanley Weston's country home is only as far West as Western New York State—so Constant's approach evokes an early pioneer settlement in its decorations. The resulting mix of Old World and American antiques would be very appropriate for a home on the heartland prairie that stretches from the Appalachian ridges to the Rocky Mountains.

Look closer at the mix and you'll see that surface textures in both bedrooms are either rough and rustic or smooth and civilized. This begs the question: What items should be rustic, and should not? Constant answers the question in a practical way in the summer bedroom. The rough-hewn beams for the bed frame are set off by soft and comfortable bedding in low-weave cottons, and homespun curtains are hung on polished brass rings. In the winter bedroom, the smooth and reflective surface of the gold-and-ebony bedstead looks quite majestic against the stained planking walls.

GEORGETTE MOSBACHER

By the Sea

ENTREPRENEUR AND POLITICAL ACTIVIST
GEORGETTE MOSBACHER CREATED THE LA
PRAIRIE COSMETICS LINE, AND IS THE AUTHOR
OF TWO FINANCIAL GUIDES FOR WOMEN,
FEMININE FORCE AND *IT TAKES MONEY, HONEY*.

Designer Peter S. Balsam wanted to preserve outward focus during daylight hours, "to get the full impact of the views."

"Waterview" is the name of entrepreneur and author Georgette Mosbacher's home in Southampton, New York, and the view from her bedroom is in fact spectacular and panoramic. The room looks out both on a bay and on the Atlantic Ocean, and designer Peter S. Balsam wanted to preserve that outward focus during daylight hours, "to get the full impact of the views." But he also wanted to give the room a warm and intimate feeling for the evening.

So Balsam created a monochromatic bedroom in sandy tones, adding black accents for elegance. A fabric valance around the perimeter of the room conceals its motorized blackout shades.

During construction of the home, Mosbacher had weekly on-site meetings with the design team to review progress, solve problems, and plan the next stage of construction. Time was of the essence: Mosbacher wanted the work done in fall and winter so she could move in in the spring. So Balsam had to find furniture that could be delivered in weeks, not months, and select only fabrics that were readily available. Astonishingly, the installation of furnishings in the entire 6,320-square-foot house was done in one single day—but a very long one. "This entailed a carefully orchestrated scheme of organized chaos," says Balsam.

None of the chaos shows in the elegant finished product. Wrapped by sunlight, the bedroom soars fearlessly above the ever-present sea—a reflection of the personality of Mosbacher, a fiercely independent woman who is also an avid sailor.

Bedroom as luxury liner: curtainless windows expose sun, sand, and sea. The window valance hides and holds the mechanics for blackout shades.

The Design Details

PALETTE

Balsam's color plan evokes an ocean beach: white, ivory, sand, and pale blue for the walls, bedding, rugs, and chair fabrics. These same colors appear in the set of framed watercolors that depict sailing ships. Black accents, such as the carved tables and black fabric shades for the standing lamps, lend a trim, nautical touch.

What Makes the Look: Beach Essentials

Bedrooms are for sleeping, so blackout shades are an absolute necessity when bedrooms have large, view-facing windows. Typically, a layer of thin, plastic foam supplies the opacity and is bonded to duck-cloth or other sturdy fabric. You can find both cloth draperies and pull-down shades with a blackout fabric in standard window sizes (63, 72, and 90 inch [1.6, 1.8, and 2.3 m]) from retail stores and catalogs that carry a large selection of off-the-shelf window treatments.

FROM JOANNA'S JOURNAL

Commercially made blackout shades are usually available in just one color—beige. That's just fine, because you wouldn't want dark-colored window treatments in a room like this, so dedicated to sun and air.

Room
With a View

STANLEY GALLIN IS A HOLLYWOOD PRO-
DUCER (*BUFFY THE VAMPIRE SLAYER*)
AND MANAGER (MICHAEL JACKSON,
DOLLY PARTON, MARIAH CAREY).

"When you sit up in bed, you can see [the ocean] through a large pair of sliding doors," says designer Bill Lane.

Just as the changing tides slowly change the profile of the Malibu beach that sit below his bedroom balcony, Sandy Gallin has often been moved to change and experiment with his living quarters. Bill Lane has been his designer through many such journeys, and at least five beach houses.

"Tailored" is the adjective that comes to mind for the earlier version. Gallin wanted a white-on-white color plan as a backdrop for his collections of antique furniture, art glass, and photographs. The very dark teak-colored floors helped set off a colorful area rug that is one of Gallin's favorites. The William Morris-style rug "was used as the only color accent except for the accessories," says Lane, who also came up with an unusual solution to the problem of where to put the television. In this bedroom, the set descended from the ceiling for viewing from the bed.

The newer bedroom also came with a wonderful view of the Pacific Ocean that dictated part of the design: "When you sit up in bed, you can see it through a large

pair of sliding doors," says Lane. Mechanical shutters were built onto the outside of the house, with soffits made to blend in with the existing architecture. "This allowed the windows to remain unobstructed during the day, with no cumbersome window treatments," says Lane.

Gallin decided to maintain the white-on-white color scheme. Both the old and new bedrooms required lots of storage for books and memorabilia. While the older room had traditional shelving, in the newer one the wall shelving was modernized for a sleeker look. An upholstered bench now sits at the foot of the bed, and extra seating was added to make the room more available as a living space.

The upholstery is still a white cotton twill that "needed to be rather dog-proof," says Lane. Gallin is fond of dogs, and a small pack of Boston terriers have the run of the house. Not surprisingly, the colorful rug seen in the early photos was recently retired, and Lane replaced it with a larger carpet in a traditional pattern that adds warmth and enhances the sleeker style of the bedroom.

Bedroom, redesign: an oriental-style rug replaces the William Morris design. The sleigh bed is raised on matching wooden blocks so an ocean view can be enjoyed while reclining. The collection of dog photographs was taken by a talented friend, well-known portrait photographer Herb Ritts.

Bedroom, before: Elements of style that were retained included the cherry wood sleigh bed, low wooden table, casual armchairs, and a favorite Tiffany lamp.

The Design Details

PALETTE
White-on-white, with dark accents.

THE BED AND BEDDING
The cherry wood sleigh bed is a extra-large king ("California king") size bed from the Richelieu Collection.

FURNISHINGS
The antique English bench by the bed and a low French table in the seating area were discovered at Hideaway House Antiques in Los Angeles. Slipcovered chairs are by Shabby Chic. The new rug is from Mansour, also in Los Angeles. The Tiffany lamp is the real thing, one of several owned by Gallin and displayed throughout his home.

Wooden shutters for the balcony's French doors are typical window treatments and used instead of curtains in both homes.

What Makes the Look: Deciding What to Keep

Redecorating poses problems for everyone, even media moguls. Sandy Gallin's collection of traditional furnishings includes some items he will probably keep for a lifetime—such as the Tiffany glass lamps—as well as the practical cotton twill slipcovers that can be easily replaced.

Moving items from room to room puts them in a fresh perspective. If you can't bear to get rid of a collectible, move it rather than squirrel it away. Rearrange photos on a wall in different ways, or switch photographs from wall frames to table frames, and vice versa.

White-on-white can be tricky in a room: it can look cold unless it's filled to bursting with personal objects or lots of books. Colorful rugs add warmth.

ADRIENNE VITTADINI

Nesting Instinct

ADRIENNE VITTADINI IS A MANHATTAN-BASED FASHION DESIGNER.

"I began this room with a vision of a peaceful environment in cool neutrals: ivory, cream, taupe, and white," says Adrienne Vittadini.

Opposite: Crisp white linen finds its airy echo in a parchment-covered armoire, a Jean-Michel Frank design reproduction from Holly Hunt that seems equally weightless. Vittadini found the squat wooden stools in Venice, and had them covered in fur.

Adrienne Vittadini's trend-setting designs often begin with her own preferences for shapes and materials. "Your bedroom should be a place of nesting, the most intimate space in your home," says fashion designer Adrienne Vittadini. Her Manhattan home is a nest that is perched pretty high, and "has such an incredible view " of city skyline and the broad expanse of a body of water—the Central Park reservoir—that Vittadini's first step in designing the bedroom was to have larger windows installed. "With no details to distract," she adds, "We wanted to enjoy the beautiful natural light and the vista."

One brilliant idea for her "nest in the sky" was to place padding on all walls before covering them with linen fabric. This treatment also made it possible to create some badly needed storage room—closet space for her husband—which was concealed behind the padded walls.

"I began this room with a vision of a peaceful environment in cool neutrals: ivory, cream, taupe, and white," she says. To assemble the elements, she first put together a "mood board"—a kind of storyboard designers often use for inspiration, combining fabric swatches and pictures. "My good friend and fellow designer Larry Laslo helped bring the concept to the room."

Vittadini prefers natural and organic fabrics and used them throughout the room, padding the headboard with the same linen fabric. For contrast, she installed dark ebony nightstands on either side of the bed and upholstered two antique wooden stools in spotted pony skin. A parchment-covered armoire adds a crisp note.

Much of the furniture is treasure from a lifetime interest in "modern and classic" furnishings. "I'm a collector and many of my favorite pieces are in this room," Vittadini says. "It is an interesting blend of strong and soft . . . and it gives me such an inner peace."

The Design Details

THE BED AND FABRICS

Vittadini designed the headboard in taupe linen, which was also used to border a darker shade of the same fabric for the bed skirt and pleated roman window shades. The bed linens are from Frette, and were purchased in Milan. Carpeting is a "fine handloom from France" that she had sewn together for wall-to-wall coverage.

FURNISHINGS

"I prefer my bedroom to be dominated by things that I love—books and art, not by a strong palette," says Vittadini. Pride of place is given to the quartet of seventeenth-century Old Master drawings mounted in matching gold frames above the bed, and a Picasso drawing she purchased at Christie's.

What Makes the Look: Floating on a Cloud

In this small bedroom, padded walls and the cloud-like bed, with its pure white linens, create a restful sanctuary. Padding the walls does not make the room seem smaller; rather, carpeting in the same linen shade as the walls creates a seamless environment built around purity of color and line.

MARY HIGGINS
CLARK

Victorian
Garden

"We produced this wonderful airy space," says designer Eve Ardia, "true to the integrity of the architecture."

Many writers want their living spaces to be a quiet retreat. Author Mary Higgins Clark also wanted hers to be a place where her grandchildren could feel at home. Her summer house in Spring Lake, New Jersey, is a restored 1880's Victorian updated with modern comforts and big, light-filled windows, romantically dressed with period details by her designer, Eve Ardia.

Ardia's cottage garden motif, expressed in the bedrooms, is a Victorian floral fantasy, with beautiful fabrics and soft window treatments. A grass-green rug and enough white beadboard to stand in for a white picket fence are some of the elements that give the entire house the aura of a sunny springtime garden. "We produced this wonderful airy space," says Ardia, "true to the integrity of the architecture."

Above: Turquoise blue seems perfect for a bedroom by the sea.

Right: Mary Higgins Clark's gilt dressing table and mirror are from Carver's Guild—The Carol Canner Collection. The sterling silver dresser set and antique lamp are family heirlooms.

What Makes the Look: Dressy Details

Throughout the rooms, small details create flowery effects. Try to imagine the bay window valance without the old-fashioned ball fringe, for example, or the dressing table mirror without its matching side bows. A high-ceilinged bathroom was given a fresh look with tromp l'oeil flowerpots; the curtain trim in the same bathroom picks up the same colors as the bands of colored tile below.

The Design Details

WINDOW TREATMENTS

Large window areas can be a challenge to dress in a feminine style. Ardia's solution gracefully assembles the necessary elements: a narrow ruffled valance balanced horizontally by the window shades in a complementary shade of peach. The shades do more than shield the sun; they visually divide the broad expanse of glass. This makes the windows less extreme and less dominant in the room. The window fabric, which was also used for matching bed pillows, is "Floral Cartouche" from Cowtan & Tout.

The wallpaper is "Powdered Aqua" from Schumacher.

FURNISHINGS

A few antiques, reproductions, and heirlooms add a period flavor. The small white writing desk is mid-twentieth-century French provincial style; the kidney-shaped dressing table and mirror are French reproductions from the Carver's Guild in Massachusetts. The hip-high Victorian-style bathtub is a Kohler Vintage K-700, a welcome destination after a day at the beach.

Above: A guest bedroom for grandchildren has its own literary inspiration— the floral wallpaper is "Edith Wharton" by Schumacher. The iron beds and the quilts are from Pottery Barn. The grassy green rug is from Hallmark Floor Company.

The master bathroom has high paneling for an airy look. Flowerpot decorations are by local New Jersey artist Margaret Patterson. The chandelier with hand-painted flowers and candle fixtures comes from Shades of Light, in Richmond, Virginia.

Romantic Retreats

A timeless tapestry, soulfully sumptuous materials, a very big and beckoning bed—romance is easy to add to any bedroom style. The rooms and suites that follow may not always be big in scale but are big-hearted by intent. All incorporate a generous inclusion of family mementos and plenty of comfortable places that let family members relax in style.

Above: A sleigh bed and down comforter add a soft touch.

Left: Philanthropist Blaine Trump's dreamy canopy.

THE LATE DIANA, PRINCESS OF WALES.

DIANA,
PRINCESS
OF WALES

A Moment
in Time

"The goal," says interior designer Ron Wilson, "was to create a safe haven."

After her divorce from England's Prince Charles in 1996, Diana, Princess of Wales, attempted to resume a private life, supported by her many friends and admirers. Dodi Fayed, the department store heir, purchased this Malibu Beach villa for Diana as their romantic getaway destination. Nestled into five secluded acres, the estate was previously owned by actor Julie Andrews and her husband, film producer Blake Edwards. An interim owner tore down the main house and replaced it with a European-style home, under the supervision of legendary Hollywood designer Ron Wilson, who saw to the custom interior furnishings as well. Fayed bought the home and all its contents in 1997, intending this bedroom to be Diana's private sanctuary.

Wilson's interpretation of these most intimate rooms, the master bedroom and adjacent dressing suite, still powerfully evokes the mood of a loving embrace.

With maximum privacy in mind, the bedroom was given shuttered windows, and its walls were softly upholstered in beige raw silk taffeta. A deeper escape, into the bed itself, was suggested by using a heavy-textured gauze that draped voluminously on all its sides of its metal frame.

Says Wilson, "The goal was to create a safe haven. I want each room to give the feeling that it is wrapping its arms around you."

This romantic sentiment extends to the dressing bathroom, where an architecturally significant window seems to hug and shelter the deep double bathtub. Limestone walls and cut marble tiles show a strong European influence in the decor, adding a unique sense of historical weight to the general outlines of a California villa.

Diana never enjoyed this serene retreat; she and Dodi Fayed died together in a car crash in Paris in 1997.

"Unfortunately, they never lived in it together," notes Wilson. "For one of the most beloved women in the world, this dream home shall forever remain exactly that—a dream."

Above: The blond side of beige, softened nearly into ivory, is the main color cue. "A beautiful backdrop for her," says Wilson. Secluded under roof beams, the metal bed, which was designed by Wilson, can be its own hideaway when drapes of "Treebark" gauze are drawn.

Right: The finest materials, elegance and restraint seem to typify the Wilson touch: details in the dressing bath include a rock crystal chandelier by Paul Ferrante and an antique Kilim area rug from Christie's Auction House. The imported tiles come from Country Floors and the marble from Renaissance Marble.

Abundant windows bring the outdoors in, setting the mood for dinners and conversations by candlelight—or sunset.

The Design Details

WALL AND WINDOW TREATMENTS

Wall panels of softly padded, raw-silk taffeta add calming quiet to this room; the fabric is by Clarence House (see Sources). Any more drapery would have been out of place, given the relaxed furniture in the seating area upholstered in hand woven chenille, and the billowy gauze used with the bed. The plain shutters in the bedroom suit the casual post-and-beam construction of the room far better. In the dressing-bathroom, the tall window looks out only upon a small courtyard's wall fountain and so could remain uncurtained for maximum light.

This dramatic staircase leads to the master bedrooms on the second floor. Stair risers are Italian-inspired tiles from Country Floors. The Buddha is a Chinese antique.

What Makes the Look: Softly Modern

As with Patti LaBelle's bedroom (see pages 12-15), this design relies much on restrained elegance and neutral colors to provide a serene setting amid the harsh light of California sunshine, and an escape from the often-harsher light of celebrity. But beige here has a blonder look, and the furniture itself seems to float as part of the backdrop. Black accents of the iron bed, the low iron table, and the bathroom's tile and tub trim pull these functional areas into focus.

FROM JOANNA'S JOURNAL

As these rooms show, both men and women experience a desire for serene, secluded, romantic bedroom retreats. Being treated like a princess (or a prince) is something we can and should do for ourselves. Find the time and space to create your own dream, to add to your peaceful rest and your enjoyment of life.

Timeless Toile

THE ALLURING SANDRA McCONNELL IS A VIBRANT MOVER IN NEW YORK SOCIAL CIRCLES AND A CHAMPION OF ANIMAL RESCUE CHARITIES.

"It's a warm, cozy, and elegant place," says designer Josef Pricci. "It's what Sandra is all about."

One obvious route to a bedroom that is cozy and intimate—but one rarely used by our celebrities—is to have a small bedroom. That is just what entrepreneur Sandra McConnell decided she wanted. McConnell—whose late husband, Neil, and his family founded Avon Products, Inc.—lives in a large house in Southampton, New York. But she chose the smallest room in the home as her master suite. The result: "It's a warm, cozy and elegant place," says designer Josef Pricci. "It's what Sandra is all about."

The room itself, Pricci says, "is perfectly square—a designer's dream. And it has plenty of light, with many windows that face the terrace." The room is completely decorated in a pale blue-and-white toile, reminiscent of rooms McConnell once stayed in in Europe. The walls' French toile fabric was made in Paris, copied from an eighteenth-century pattern. The furniture is genuine eighteenth-century, from England—including the canopy bed. Above the canopy, the ceiling is mirrored. This multiplies the effect of the toile and reflects the beauty of the Pratesi linens. "It helps give the toile a light feeling," Pricci says. Even the carpeting is blue and white.

McConnell has a large collection of dog paintings, some of them placed here in the bedroom. She is active in animal rescue and also has her own pet dogs. Naturally, they have their own dog bed—in toile. "It's a miniature version of her own bed," says Pricci.

What Makes the Look: Feminine Fabric

French toile de Jouy is a time-less look, and women of all ages are attracted to it. Because we love it so much, there's an urge to indulge in a total look. Going over the top with toile is completely appropriate when reclaiming this comforting, elegant, and rich-looking style for your own bedroom. Don't stint on toile, for it is a feminine fabric that envelopes yet is not overbearing even when used everywhere in a room.

Toiles are easy to find in classic blue and red; less common green toile is particularly stun-ning, while black toile makes such a powerful statement it is often used for dining rooms and living rooms as well as in bed-rooms.

The best toile de Jouy fabrics are hand-blocked and crisply rendered upon a pale, creamy-white background. So-called "modern" toile de Jouy, on a gold background, is a terribly formal look that can seem oppressive when used in wallpaper.

Manufacturers of toile bed linens generally supply match-ing fabric accessories, such as window treatments, lamp-shades, and desk sets.

Mixing patterns does not work so well: many designers will add a check or a striped fabric in a matching color to round out a room. If you can't find wallpaper to match a toile pattern that you love, order enough extra fabric to cover one wall (such as the wall behind a headboard) for a finished look.

Above: This Southampton bedroom is awash in French toile de Jouy: comforter, bed skirt, bed canopy, armchair, and wallpaper all in the same pattern.

Left: Designer Joseph Price flouts the oft-repeated advice to display toile de Jouy fabric flat, to empha-size the pattern images. His choice to generously ruffle and shirr the fabric magnifies its opulence and femininity. Pillow coverings and bed linens are by Pratesi.

MICKEY ROURKE

Gilded Glamour

"Mickey wanted it to look like a New Orleans hotel suite, or an ancient and grand Paris hotel," says designer David W. Purdie.

Angels are everywhere in Mickey Rourke's Manhattan pied-a-terre. Cherubs and Italian putti in paint, plaster, gilt, bronze, and gold are the protective spirits for an actor best known for powerful screen roles (*Barfly*, *9 ½ Weeks*, *Angel Heart*, *Wild Orchid*). The words "romantic, dramatic, and over-the-top" often describe his performances, and they apply in full measure to the grand elegance of this bedroom, created and furnished in eighteenth-, nine-teenth-, and twentieth-century antiques by David W. Purdie.

"Mickey wanted it to look like a New Orleans hotel suite, or an ancient and grand Paris hotel," says Purdie. "He's a multifaceted person, and with every one of his residences he attempts a design that's architec-turally appropriate so he can experience different styles of living." In a previous home, for example, Rourke had commissioned Native American artists to paint murals in a southwestern genre.

This bedroom was originally the living room. Purdie notes the build-ing was already blessed with parquet floors and 14-foot (4.3 m) ceilings,

and its affinity to an authentic hotel mood is perhaps no accident (the nineteenth-century brownstone was designed by Henry Hardenbergh, the architect for New York's venerable Plaza Hotel.) He started on wall treatments, looked for *putti* every-where, and began what would be a long search for the beautiful furnish-ings that would re-create the romantic glamour of a European Grand Hotel in each of the rooms.

"After two months of calling all the best dealers of fine antiques in New Orleans and Paris, and not finding anything—I thought I would go to this local furniture warehouse in the New York area," says Purdie. "I was told there was nothing for me but I went through the rooms anyway, and stumbled upon this fantastic bed. It was a new shipment that had just arrived that day. I called Mickey—apprehensively—and he agreed to show up within the hour. He fell in love with the bed, and with all the other pieces, which were of the same style. We agreed to buy all the pieces, and at that point I began to relax about the project."

The strong, deep colors shown here lend a masculine feeling to the elaborate decoration. A plain painted ceiling in soft terra cotta, the expanse of polished wood flooring, and the broad dark wall borders keep the patterns from overwhelming.

The Design Details

PALETTE

According to Purdie, Rourke had a clear vision for the dark jewel tones —deep lapis blue, rich coral-reds, and glowing amber-golds that decorate the walls and carpeting. One source of inspiration was his visit to Gianni Versace's lakeside villa in Italy, which included midnight-blue walls in a color scheme straight out of a Titian painting (for Versace bedrooms in Miami, see page 16). Gold detailing, to match the gilded and metal carvings of the furniture, was used throughout the apartment.

BED AND FURNITURE

A starring role is given to the Italian Revival bed, an import that dates from the early to mid twentieth century (circa 1940). The wide headboard is fitted with globe lights (replaced by Purdie with amber glass) and brass insets showing anatomically correct cupids at play. A mirrored chest from the same suite of furniture also has globe lamps and brass panels. The desk on the opposite side of the room is not part of the suite, but is nineteenth century and similar in style thanks to gilt carvings and inlay.

WALL PAINT AND COVERINGS

Panels of navy blue and pale coral velvet silk damask were given wide molding frames, washed in gold, and are set off by broad borders of dark blue walls painted in faux lapis-lazuli. Like the true lapis stone, which is used as an oil paint pigment and for jewelry, the walls are slightly veined and have a high gloss to reflect light.

WINDOWS AND LIGHTING

It always seems to be twilight here—a common problem in New York brownstones. Purdie and Rourke took this cue to create a romantic glow with amber globes and the bedside cherub lamps with alabaster shades. A crystal chandelier became the dominant light source once Rourke decided to change the window treatment, replacing the shutters shown here with leopard-spotted velvet draperies that matched a new duvet, and added a navy blue window shade.

What Makes the Look: The Gilt Edge

Italian Revival furniture may be difficult to find outside of major cities. Italian bedroom suites built after World War II tend to be less elaborate, but can be adapted by adding ornamentation with drawer-pull tassels in golden silk and accessories in ormolu. Nineteenth-century French styles lavish with gold-painted detailing can also conjure up the romantic setting of a European Grand Hotel.

The gold-washed molding that surrounds the wall panels brightens and defines the dark colors. In a smaller bedroom, mounting gold-colored picture frames on a dark blue painted wall can approximate this quickly and easily. Sample it first and decide how you like the look before going all the way.

Deeply colored bedding and draperies can get their own gleam if you sew on gold fringe and tassels. Thick, golden, silk ropes can be curtain tiebacks or be romantically looped across the top of a mirror.

Dark painted walls need lots of lighting. Don't stint on brass and gilt lamps and reflective accessories such as ormolu clocks, brass-bound boxes, and golden candleholders.

FROM JOANNA'S JOURNAL
Mixing furniture from different styles and historical periods is a lot easier if you select a theme. Besides angels and cupids, furniture decorated with golden lion heads (with the mouth open and a wavy mane) is ubiquitous throughout European design.

Brass cherub carvings on the bed and chest.

Below: Bedroom as adventure: swashbuckling furniture re-creates the romantic look of old European hotels and New Orleans. Faux lapis walls are a cool counterpoint to the luxurious use of gold accessories and gold furniture. The fireplace and moldings came with the room; the desk is nineteenth-century French with gilt inlay.

JOAN RIVERS

A Softer Side

STANDUP COMIC, TALK SHOW HOSTESS, CABLE
SHOPPING ICON, CELEBRITY AUTHOR AND
FASHION EXPERT, THE DYNAMIC JOAN RIVERS
HAS AN ELEGANT HOME FOR OFFSTAGE HOURS.

"The canopy bed has Swiss lace hanging from it, making it look very romantic," says designer Louis Malkin.

This bedroom is Joan Rivers's favorite room in her New York apartment. No wonder, according to its designer, Louis Malkin, who has decorated five homes for and with Rivers. He says: "It's very feminine, just like her."

Best known for her incisive wit, the comedian, talk show host, and author has her tranquil side. "The canopy bed has Swiss lace hanging from it, making it look very romantic, says Malkin. "The windows are also surrounded by Swiss lace. And she has fresh-cut flowers every day—roses, soft pale peach and pink ones."

In many ways, the bedroom looks like an indoor garden. "All her other bedrooms were very formal," Malkin says. "This time she wanted a complete change, a garden look, to match the beautiful terrace and garden outside her bedroom window."

Malkin's interpretation of the garden look leans heavily on his inspired wall design. The bottom trim of the walls is painted green, to look like grass. Above, there is hand-painted wallpaper, with branches, birds, butterflies, flowers, and leaves. The pattern is a custom design by Gracie Wallpaper, a New York company that has specialized in handmade oriental wall coverings for nearly 100 years. The wallpaper covers the ceiling, doors, and closets, so you cannot tell the doors from the walls—making it easy for Rivers to enfold herself in an intimate, personal indoor paradise.

Yet this garden has some features not to be found outdoors—like the fireplace that Malkin had built in marble, from a Louis XV design. Rivers keeps the fireplace going nearly all year long. Other endearments are lots of family pictures in silver frames—and a tiny, upholstered stairway by the bed, so her beloved dog can climb up to sleep.

Imported Swiss lace drapes
the canopy bed and hides
task lighting mounted
beneath the canopy, aug-
menting the bedside lamps
in porcelain and peach-
colored silk.

The Design Details

PALETTE
According to Malkin, River's favorite color is peach. The dominant color in the wallpaper is a very pale peach, with a design that has highlights of taupe, blue, lavender, and salmon-pink.

"The wallpaper originally came in too light," notes Malkin. So it was hand painted to add more vibrant colors to the birds, flowers, leaves, and butterflies. When this was finished, the wallpaper was glazed all over to give it an antique look, "as if it had been there for years," says Malkin.

FURNISHINGS
Rivers favors timeless European classics, softly rendered here. Her canopy bed is enrobed in lace; a traditional French Louis XV side chair is luxuriously covered in peach-colored satin. Because she loves to read in bed—and even writes her own books there—her designer was challenged to accommodate bright reading lights in the middle of this very romantic setting.

"There are two lights, one on either side of her bed, which are concealed by the canopy bed's hanging lace," says Malkin. "They are very small, twin halogen lights on brackets that can extend out 30 inches (76 cm), and they can be swung back when not being used."

WINDOW FABRICS AND BEDDING
Airy lengths of imported Swiss lace drape the windows as well as the canopy bed. A white satin duvet and embroidered lace coverlet were made to order, with matching linens and pillow shams.

FLOOR TREATMENT
Because the room is quite small, the floors were fully covered in a pale, patterned French carpeting. A section was cut out to accommodate the polished marble hearth tiles in front of the fireplace.

Opposite: Try to imagine this room without wallpaper, which adds a feminine feeling to the strong lines of a marble fireplace and picture frame, all in Louis XV style.

Right: A detail of the wallpaper, showing hand-painted highlights in coral, taupe and lavender-blue.

What Makes the Look:
Work It With Wallpaper

Joan Rivers' wallpaper pattern is a custom design, not quite Chinoiserie, but typically French: a pale shade with a delicate, naturalistic pattern. Similar designs and reproductions of antique wallpapers are available. To match this look, choose a vertical pattern with a curvy branch or ribbon motif. Wallpaper with stripes or medallion designs will look too stiff and formal.

When doors and ceiling are also covered with the wallpaper, monotony will set in unless you add a strong architectural element. In this bedroom, a main wall gains the bulk of a marble fireplace surround and the gravity of a portrait in an extra-large oval frame. If you can't fit a fireplace into your room, consider adding an overmantel in ornately carved wood to use as a wall shelf, or hang a large mirror with a strongly architectural frame.

Adding hand-painted highlights to wallpaper is not difficult, but it does require patience and a steady hand. Use acrylic paints, diluted with water, and fine camelhair brushes, and practice first on a spare part of a roll. Alternatively, trace a stencil on your wallpaper design, and use the cutout template and a sponge to add color in a uniform way to the pattern. Seal the color with a glaze for a perfect finish.

The Royal Treatment

NASCAR RACING LEGEND JUNIOR JOHNSON AND FAMILY.

Lisa Johnson had considerable input into the design, too says Dowell. "One of Lisa's requests was whatever you do, make it one of a kind and romantic!"

NASCAR auto racing legend Junior Johnson waited a long time to build his dream home. When it was time to build a bedroom for his North Carolina home, Johnson and his wife, Lisa, wanted it to be as heroic as the rest of the Georgian-style mansion they had built from hand-made brick on their 600-acre cattle ranch—within a few miles of where they both grew up.

"It was obvious immediately to me how a simple country boy could become one of NASCAR's biggest legends," says designer Leo Dowell. "Junior wanted to know every detail—and how each could be improved."

Lisa Johnson had considerable input into the design, too, says Dowell. "One of Lisa's requests was whatever you do, make it one of a kind and romantic!"

Dowell's responding royal treatment extends to the adjacent master bath, which is decorated with a ceiling of blue sky and trompe l'oeil brick and contains a limestone circular shower, heated floors, a three-way mirror, and a window seat.

Another request—one that drove Dowell around the world to search for just the right pieces for this room—was to "make this a home we will always want to come back to." Dowell was able to do his world-wide search for furnishings in high style—"through several trips via one of the Johnsons' personal King airplanes." The result, says Dowell, is "fit for a King and Queen of racing."

This "royal" bedroom suite isn't a matched set: each item is one-of-a-kind but in the same colors. The height of the bedposts is extreme, so it needs its companion, the padded bench, to bring it down to earth (or at least down to carpet) with a graduated visual rhythm.

The Design Details

PALETTE

Nugget gold and cream are the colors for the damask bedding, bed skirt, draperies, and upholstery. The same tones appear in the painted wood furniture, and in the customized cabinetry for the master bath. A fine expanse of cocoa-colored silk, against a cocoa-toned wall, makes a fitting backdrop for the glittering gold accents.

Gilt-and-cream cabinets in the master bath are fronts for modern built-ins, provided by Dowell to continue the overall Georgian atmosphere of this home.

What Makes the Look: A Draped Wall

Heavy silk in a cocoa-brown has an iridescent shimmer that recalls the tapestry and arras once deployed in ancient castles to keep out drafts. Here it provides a visual warmth to the creamy furnishings. The cloth is hung from ornament hooks from the wall's top molding, and this creates a three-dimensional effect that might not have been achieved by arranging the draperies on a rod.

Window treatments are similarly formal, with in cream-and-gold silk brocade to match the coverlet.

FROM JOANNA'S JOURNAL

You don't have to live in a Southern mansion to drape a bedroom wall. A good friend who lives on Manhattan's Sutton Place recently planned a similar treatment for her bedroom—with shirred fabric behind her antique sleigh bed—to conceal slight flaws in the finish of her built-in wall cabinets, and help soundproof her New York apartment.

BLAINE TRUMP

Lavender Dreams

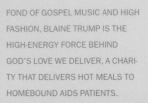

The room is romantic, highly styled, and yet comfortable, reflecting Trump's joy in entertaining and representing her success as one of New York's great hostesses.

A small and beautiful fantasy bedroom was designed by Greg Jordan for philanthropist Blaine Trump in New York City. She picked the color: lavender. He found the perfect fabric—a rare shade of lavender French toile showing scenes of Paris—and this bedroom fantasy took wing.

The room is romantic, highly styled and yet comfortable, reflecting Trump's joy in entertaining and representing her success as one of New York's great hostesses. Amazingly, this is a guest bedroom—designed so every need a guest might have while staying there is met. It is filled with personal touches: odds and ends collected by Trump from her own shopping trips and travels. For example, the framed images of Paris that decorate the headboard are simply vintage postcards, an endearing detail. The room was also given some unique touches from Jordan, like the Scottish lace in the bed, which he embellished with a custom fringe hung with amethyst and crystal beads.

The room is small—Jordan had to scale the pieces to accommodate real-size people without violating the proportions of the architecture. A slipper chair and painted wood secretary are quite small, and make the bed seem bigger by comparison. It all feels like a fantasy, Jordan says: "Sleeping in the bed is like being in a cloud."

Above: Country French touches include the Sèvres plates as wall decor, glass hurricane lamp by the window, and a rustic basket for logs between the fireplace and slipper chaise.

Right: Many yards of fine white Scottish lace have been further embellished with amethyst beads. Bed, headboard, and custom bedding are all by Greg Jordan.

What Makes the Look: A Different Look on Toile

The same toile patterns that look refreshingly crisp in traditional blue and white turn out to be hauntingly romantic when rendered in this unusual shade of amethyst purple. Compared to the McConnell bedroom (see page 129), this is a French version of toile, using delicate painted furniture instead of the substantial George III chests found in English interiors.

WANDA
FERRAGAMO

Feminine
Tour de Force

The feminine combination of pink and green becomes a high-fashion statement when rendered in celery and soft peach.

As head of a high-fashion house that spans several continents, Wanda Ferragamo asked designer Dennis Rolland to give her a "tranquil retreat" in her high-rise apartment above New York's Fifth Avenue. Rolland responded with his vision— "a small Italian palazzo within a modern New York apartment building"—and she placed the details confidently within his hands.

"Mrs. Ferragamo spent a few days in November working with me, and we selected the major fabrics, the wallpaper, and the carpets," says Rolland. "Then she went back to Italy and wouldn't be back until the following May, when the apartment had to be completed." Before she left, she deputized her daughter-in-law, who lives in New York full time, to continue to work with the

designer as he chose the furniture for her, and completed the elegant treatments for the windows and the bed. All six of her children work in the family fashion empire started by her late husband, Salvatore, who died in 1960. Wanda is chairman of the board.

Rolland kept couture in mind in his fabric work, matching the custom cloth of the upholstery, curtains, bed hangings, dust ruffle, and bedspread with detailed trimming that includes piping, passementerie, and fringe.

"When she walked in the door, she was thrilled," says Rolland. "Especially with all the dressmaker details, such as the special linings for the curtains—just like a fashion designer would do in a couture coat."

Above: A feminine carpet by
Stark sets the mood, as does a
regal corona headboard. The patterned silk pillows on the bed are
a Ferragamo scarf fabric.

Right: Elegant furnishings
include this richly inlaid antique
credenza, used as a bureau and
dressing table.

The Design Details

PALETTE
The feminine combination of pink and green becomes a high-fashion statement when rendered in celery and soft peach.

THE BED AND BEDDING
The corona canopy headboard is a Louis XVI innovation, one that gives this room its focal point. The luxurious printed fabric used for the canopy, bed curtains, padded headboard, and bed skirt is by Osborne & Little; the heavy pink silk used for the coverlet is from Brunschwig & Fils.

WALL AND WINDOW COVERINGS
Wallpaper and window curtain fabric is available through Rose Cumming of New York, and the work was done in the studios of La Regence. The Fifth Avenue view is framed with heavy drapes and a short valance with a long insert, over sheer curtains that tumble ever so slightly onto the floor. The designer also added the crown moldings, painted a bright white, that give the room additional height.

LIGHTING
No overhead lamps, but soft pools of light that flow from lamps placed everywhere. Sconce shelving is purely decorative, used here for candles and art glass.

FURNISHINGS
Rolland selected a mix of antiques and reproductions. Opposite the bed is a credenza dating from the nineteenth century. The chairs are modern and upholstered in geometric green velvet that matches the passementerie on the curtains. The French figure lamps are from Marvin Alexander in New York but many other objects are sweet souvenirs.

"She collects antique perfume bottles, some of which you can see on the credenza," says Rolland of his client, whose personality hovers in the room, like a perfume, during the months she resides in Italy or is traveling her fashion empire.

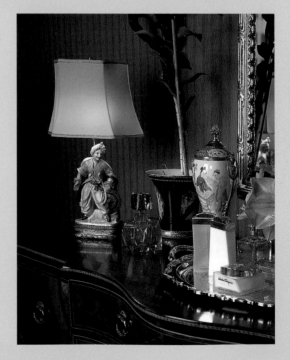

French paste porcelain lamp and Chinese import china, found by the designer in New York.

What Makes the Look:
Mixing Fabric Patterns

Dressmaker details are only part of the inspired fabric treatments that make this bedroom a Dennis Rolland tour de force. The Stark carpet itself is a fashion statement, custom colored to the exact shade of peach-pink. The floral fabric used for the bedding is a well-spaced, quiet pattern—it doesn't fight the carpet. The very soft tones of the celery-and-peach-striped satin on the bench provide an additional visual transition from bed to floor.

Large planes of color, in the single-note curtains, table skirts, and bedspread, keep the mood airy and light. The choice of fabric-covered round tables helps considerably and creates a better effect than bedside tables in dark wood.

Linings and passementerie can be sewn into your own curtains to add a finishing touch. The deep green trim on the window valance, for example, creates an elegant line that will be effective when the curtains are open, or drawn closed.

FROM JOANNA'S JOURNAL
A corona headboard can be assembled with a curved curtain rod, mounted to the ceiling above a bed. To determine the measurements for a size that is in scale to your bed, consider the side of the bed first. A twin bed can probably get away with standard 84-inch (2.1 m) draperies; anything larger will require a custom length to reach the floor on either side.

She'll take Manhattan: a view of the city provides inspiration and perspective.

Resources

ABC CARPET
881 Broadway
New York, NY 10003, USA
(212) 473-3000

AMERICAN COUNTRY COLLECTION
53 Old Santa Fe Trail
Santa Fe, NM 87501, USA
(505) 982-1296

ANDRE DE CACQUERAY
227 Ebury Street
London SW1W 8UT
England
(0171) 730 5000

ANICHINI
230 Fifth Avenue
New York, NY 10001, USA
(212) 679-9540

and

ANICHINI
466 N. Robertson Boulevard
West Hollywood, CA 90048, USA
(310) 657-4292

ARTE DE MEXICO
5356 Riverton Avenue
North Hollywood, CA 91601, USA
(818) 769-5090

B&J FABRICS
263 West 40th Street
New York, NY 10018, USA
(212) 354-8150

HILARY BATSTONE ANTIQUES
8 Holbein Place
London SW1
England
(020) 7730 5335

GEOFFREY BENNISON
16 Holbein Place
London SW1
England
(020) 7730 8076

and

BENNISON
Fine Arts Building
232 East 59th Street
New York, NY 10022, USA
(212) 223-0373

BERBERE IMPORTS
3049 S La Cienega Boulevard
Culver City, CA 90232, USA
(310) 842-3842

LA BOUTIQUE DES JARDINS
Boulevard Mirabeau
13210 St. Remy de Provence
France
(4) 90 92 11 60

BRAQUENIE
2 rue de Furstenberg
75006 Paris
France
01 46 33 73 00

BRUNSCHWIG & FILS, INC.
979 Third Avenue, 12th Floor
New York, NY 10022-1234, USA
(212) 838-7878
www. brunschwig.com

CALVIN KLEIN HOME COLLECTION
Available throughout the USA
(800) 294-7978

CENTURY FURNITURE INDUSTRIES
www.centuryfurniture.com

CHRIS PERRY WOODWORKING, INC.
55 Washington Street, Room #500
Brooklyn, NY 11201, USA
(718) 596-7185

CHRIS GIBBS
3 Dove Walk (off Pimlico Road)
London SW1
England
(020) 7730 8200

CHRISTOPHER HYLAND
979 Third Avenue, Suite 1710
New York, NY 10022, USA
(212) 688-6121

COLE & SON WALLPAPER, LTD.
Unit G10
Chelsea Harbour Design Centre
Lotts Road
London SW10 OXE
England
(0171) 376 4628

LES COUILLES DU CHIEN
65 Golborne Road
London W10
England
(020) 8968 0099

COWTAN & TOUT
979 Third Avenue, Suite 1022
New York, NY 10022, USA
(212) 753-4488

**CUSTOM TOUCH FOR
INTERIORS INC.**
17541 Collins Street
Encino, CA 91316, USA
(818) 609-8720

DAVID DUNCAN ANTIQUES
227 East 60th Street
New York, NY 10022, USA
(212) 688-0666

DAVID LINLEY'S
60 Pimlico Road
London SW1
England
(020) 7730 7300

DIAMOND FOAM AND FABRIC
611 South La Brea
Los Angeles, CA 90036, USA
(323) 931-8148

DONGHIA TEXTILES
979 Third Avenue, 6th Floor
New York, NY 10022, USA
(212) 935-3713

EDELMAN LEATHER
(800) 886-TEDY

EDWARD FIELDS INC.
232 East 59th Street
New York, NY 10022, USA
(212) 759-2200

FABRIC ADABRA
859 Ringwood Avenue
Haskell, NJ 07420, USA
(973) 839-2162

FRETTE
799 Madison Avenue
New York, NY 10021, USA
(212) 988-5221

and

FRETTE CALIFORNIA, INC.
459 N Rodeo Drive
Beverly Hills, CA 90210, USA
(310) 273- 8540

GALLERIE BLONDEEL DEROYAN
11 rue de Lille
7500 Paris
France
(1) 49 27 96 22

GIBSON STUDIO
511 La Cienega, Suite 202
Los Angeles, CA 90048, USA
(310) 659-1684

GRACIE WALLPAPER
121 West 19th Street
New York, NY 10011, USA
(212) 924-6816
www.graciestudio.com

HALLMARK FLOOR COMPANY
48 N Maple Avenue
Ridgewood, NJ 07450, USA
(201) 445-5886

HOLLY HUNT NEW YORK
979 Third Avenue
New York, NY 10022, USA
(212) 755-6555

HYDE PARK ANTIQUES
838 Broadway
New York, NY 10003, USA
(212) 477-0033

IMPORTS FROM MARRAKESH
88 Tenth Avenue
New York, NY 10011, USA
(212) 675-9700

INTERNATIONAL DOWN
8687 Melrose Avenue # 160
West Hollywood, CA 90069-5701, USA
(310) 657-8243

INTERNATIONAL SILKS AND WOOLENS
8347 Beverly Boulevard
Los Angeles, CA 90048, USA
(323) 653-6453

JEFFREY STEVENS WALLCOVERING
8687 Melrose, #B406
Los Angeles, CA 90069, USA
(310) 557-2526

J. ROBERT SCOTT
979 Third Avenue, Suite 220
New York, NY 10022, USA
(212) 755-4910

KOAN COLLECTION
6109 Melrose Avenue
Los Angeles, CA 90038, USA
(323) 464-3735

KREISS COLLECTIONS
415 N La Salle Drive
Chicago, IL 60610-4540, USA
(312) 527-0907

and

KREISS COLLECTIONS
1628 Oak Lawn Avenue
Dallas, TX 75207-3402, USA
(214) 698-9118

LEE JOFA
979 Third Avenue, Suite 234
New York, NY 10022, USA
(212) 688-0444

LIGHTING COLLABORATIVE INC.
124 West 24th Street
New York, NY 10011, USA
(212) 627-5330

LOBEL MODERN INC.
207 West 18th Street
New York, NY 10011, USA
(212) 242-9075

LYNN PALMER COLLECTION
(310) 275-6857

MISHA CARPET
18 E 53rd Street
New York, NY 10022, USA
(212) 688-5912

NOT SO FAR EAST
160 South La Brea Avenue
Los Angeles, CA 90036, USA
(323) 933-8900

OSBORNE & LITTLE
90 Commerce Road
Stamford, CT 06902, USA
(203) 359-1500

PARTRIDGE DESIGNS
10374 Mississippi Avenue
Los Angeles, CA 90025, USA
(310) 286-0152

PAVILION TEXTILES
Rushford Hall
Freshford
Bath BA3 6EJ
England
(01) 2025 722 522

PAUL FERRANTE INC
8464 Melrose Place
Los Angeles, CA 90069-5308, USA
(323) 653-4142

PINDLER & PINDLER
8687 Melrose Avenue # B530
Los Angeles, CA 90069, USA
(310) 289-0200

PORTHAULT LINENS
18 E 69th Street
New York, NY 10021, USA
(212)688-1660

POTTERY BARN
www.potterybarn.com

PRATESI LINENS INC.
829 Madison Avenue
New York, NY 10021, USA
(212) 288-2315

PRIMEWAY INDUSTRIES
33341 Dequindre Road
Troy, MI 48083-4602, USA
(248) 583-6922

PROFILES
200 Lexington Avenue # 1211
New York, NY 10016-6255, USA
(212) 689-6903

REDWING & CHAMBERS
398 Dean Street
Brooklyn, NY 11217, USA
(718) 638-4514

RICHARD MULLIGAN SUNSET COTTAGE
8157 West Sunset Boulevard
Los Angeles, CA 90046, USA
(323) 650-8660

ROBERT ALLEN
8687 Melrose Avenue # B499
Los Angeles, CA 90069, USA
(310) 659-6454

ROGERS & GOFFIGEN
979 Third Avenue
New York, NY 10022, USA
(212) 888-3242

ROSE CUMMING INC
232 E 59th Street, Floor 5
New York, NY 10022, USA
(212) 758-0844

ROSENBAUM FINE ARTS OF HOUSTON
5120 Woodway Drive # 180
Houston, TX 77056-1788, USA
(713) 622-7272

SCALAMANDRÉ
Scalamandré, Inc
8687 Melrose Avenue, B617
West Hollywood, CA 90069, USA
(310) 657 8154

and

SCALAMANDRÉ, INC
942 Third Avenue
New York, NY 10022-2701, USA
(212) 980-3888

SHERWOOD STUDIOS
6644 Orchard Lake Road
West Bloomfield, MI 48322, USA
(810) 855-1600

STARK CARPET/OLD WORLD WEAVERS
8687 Melrose Avenue, #B629
West Hollywood, CA 90069, USA
(310) 657 8275

and

3/6-7 Chelsea Harbour Design Centre
Chelsea Harbour
London, SW10 0XE
England
(020) 7352 6001

STARK CARPET CORPORATION
(212) 725-9000

**STUDIO GALDI ARCHITECTURE
AND INTERIOR DESIGN**
121 St. Marks Place
New York, NY 10009, USA
(212) 254-9348

TURKMAN GALLERY
8 Eccleston Street
London SW1
England
(020) 7730 8848

UPSTAIRS AT DIAMOND
617 South La Brea Avenue
Los Angeles, CA 90036, USA
(323) 933-5551

WAMSUTTA
1285 Avenue of the Americas
New York, NY 10019, USA
(212) 903-2000

WEST COAST TRIMMING
466 S. Robertson Boulevard
Los Angeles, CA 90048, USA
(323) 272-6569

**XAVIER LLONGUERAS/CATALONIA
COLLECTION**
1503 Cahenga Boulevard
Los Angeles, CA 90028, USA
(323) 464-5316

ZÜBER & COMPANY
979 Third Avenue
New York, NY 10022, USA
(212) 486-9226

Interior Designers

KENNETH ALPERT, I.S.I.D.
Kenneth Alpert Associates, Inc.
30 East 76th Street
New York, NY 10021, USA
(212) 535-0922

EVE ARDIA
Saddle River Interiors
67 East Allendale Avenue
Saddle River, NJ 07458, USA
(201) 934-0750

PETER S. BALSAM
1601 Third Avenue
New York, NY 10128, USA
(212) 831-6556

JOHN BARMAN
John Barman Inc.
500 Park Avenue, #14F
New York, NY 10022, USA
(212) 838-9443

MICHAEL BERMAN
Michael Berman Design
619 North Croft Avenue
Los Angeles, CA 90048, USA
(323) 655-9813

KEITH BRIAN BURNS
Design Solutions
P.O. Box 728
Palm Springs, CA 92263, USA
(760) 325-7121

CHRISTOPHER COLEMAN
70 Washington Street, Suite 1005
Brooklyn, NY 11201, USA
(718) 222-8984

GEORGE CONSTANT, A.S.I.D.
George Constant, Inc.
425 East 63rd Street
New York, NY 10021, USA
(212) 751-1907

IVAN DOLIN
Ivan Dolin Interior Design
62 Beach Street, #6B
New York, NY 10013, USA
(212) 965-9801

LEO DOWELL
Leo Dowell Interiors
501 East Morehead Street, Suite 2
Charlotte, NC 28202, USA
(704) 334-3817

MAGNUS EHRLAND
C/o Diesel S.p.A.
Via Dell' Industria 7
36060 Molvena (vi) Italia
011-39-424-477-5555
Milan: 011-39-336-333784

BEATA GALDI
Studio Galdi Architectural & Interior
Design
121 St. Marks Place
New York, NY 10009, USA
(212) 620-4092

GARY GIBSON
Gary Gibson Interior Design
511 N. La Cienega Suite 202
Los Angeles, CA 90048, USA
(310) 659-1684

ANTONIA HUTT
Antonia Hutt & Associates
755 N Kilkea Drive
Los Angeles CA 90046, USA
(323) 782-4949

GREG JORDAN
Greg Jordan, Inc.
504 East 74th Street, Suite 4W
New York, NY 10021, USA
(212) 570-4470

BILL LANE
Lane - McCook & Associates, Inc
926 North Orlando Avenue
Los Angeles, CA 90069, USA
(310) 657-7890

LOUIS MALKIN
Louis Malkin Interior Designer
148 W 23rd Street
New York, NY 10011-2435, USA
(212) 989-0377

MARK MORGANROTH, A.S.I.D.
Sherwood Studios, Inc.
6644 Orchard Lake Road
West Bloomfield, MI 48322, USA
(248) 855-1600

SANDRA NUNNERLEY, A.S.I.D.
Sandra Nunnerley Inc.
595 Madison Avenue, Suite 2300
New York, NY 10022, USA
(212) 826-0539

LYNN PALMER
Lynn Palmer Design
914 N. Roxbury Drive
Beverly Hills, CA 90210, USA
(310) 275-6857

MELISSA PARTRIDGE
Partridge Designs
10374 Mississippi Avenue
Los Angeles, CA 90025, USA
(310) 286-0152

JOSEF PRICCI
Josef Pricci, Ltd.
249 E 57th Street
New York, NY 10022, USA
(212) 486-2530

DENNIS ROLLAND
405 E 54th Street
New York, NY 10022, USA
(212) 644-0537

JACK TRAVIS
Studio J T A
Studio of Jack Travis
432 Austin Place, Floor 2
Bronx, NY 10455-5006, USA
(718) 742-6791

J. WALLACE TUTT III
Tutt Renovation & Development, Inc.
1800 Sunset Harbour Drive, Suite 3
Miami Beach, FL 33139, USA
(305) 532-8800

ALLAN WARNICK
Allan Warnick Interiors
3025 Benedict Canyon
Beverly Hills, CA 90210, USA
(310) 273-3620

RON WILSON
Ron Wilson Designer
1235 Tower Road
Beverly Hills, CA 90210, USA
(310) 276-0666

VICENTE WOLF
Vicente Wolf Associates, Inc.
333 West 39th Street
New York, NY 10018, USA
(212) 465-0590

TONY WHITFIELD
Tony Whitfield, Designer
398 Dean Street
Brooklyn, NY 11217, USA
(718) 638-4514

Photo Credits

Michael Arden: 36, 39, 41, 53
Jamie Ardiles-Arce: 51
Marianne Atkinson: 2, 60–61, 63
Maryellen Baker: 104–107
Hugh Brown: 128
Larry Brown/Courtesy of
 Junior Johnson: 138
Charles William Bush/Courtesy of
 Joan Rivers: 134
Anita Calero: 84–87
Karen Cipolla: 82, 95, 97
Courtesy of Marshall Coburn: 94
Courtesy of Derrick Coleman: 90
Grey Crawford: 13–15
Patrick DeMarchelier/Courtesy of
 Mary Tyler Moore: 64
KayLynn Deveney/Courtesy of
 Glenna Goodacre: 32
Jerry Feigelman: 83, 91
Courtesy of Wanda Ferragamo: 144
Dan Forer: 7, 10, 17–21, 58, 75, 77
Getty Images: 12, 16, 54, 68, 72, 92, 118,
 124, 130
Oberto Gili/Courtesy of *House
 Beautiful*: 117
Lynn Goldsmith/Courtesy of
 Georgette Mosbacher: 110

Douglas Hill: 25–27
Doug Kirkland/Courtesy of
 Ali MacGraw: 46
Gideon Lewin/Courtesy of Lillian
 Vernon: 22
Norman Y. Lono: 93
Roxanne Lowit: 142
Mayenfisch/Courtesy of
 Shore Fire Media: 88
Dale Mincey: 122, 143
Mary E. Nichols/Courtesy of
 Ron Wilson: 73, 125–127
Edward J. North: 23, 102, 103, 109, 129
Michael O'Neal/Courtesy of
 Corbis Images: 42
Sir Norman Parkinson/Courtesy of
 Nancy Davis: 52
Charles Pearson/Courtesy of
 Peter Vitale: 28
Rankin/Courtesy of Diesel USA: 74
Matthew Rolston/Courtesy of EMI: 38
Mark Ross: 65–67
Dennis Savini/Courtesy of
 Eve Ardia: 119–121
Durston Saylor: 43–45
Rick Scanlan: 103, 111

Carrie See/Courtesy of
 Charles Shaughnessy: 24
Pat Shanklin: 139–141
Tim Street-Porter: 6, 114–115, 123
Adrian Velicescu: 59, 69–70
Igor Vishnyakov: 145–147
Peter Vitale: 8, 11, 23, 29–31, 33–35, 37,
 47–49, 102, 109
Courtesy of Adrienne Vittadini: 116
Andreas von Einsiedel: 78–81
Dominique Vorillon: 55–57
Courtesy of S. A. Weston: 108
Charles White: 113
Timothy White/Courtesy of
 Inside Edition: 50
Robert Whitman: 98
Hal Wilson: 9, 89, 131, 133–137
Vicente Wolf: 99–100
Firooz Zahedi: 40, 112 (originally
 published in *House & Garden*)

About the Author

Joanna Lee Doster is an interior designer, an appraiser of antiques and decorative arts, and an authority of current design trends. Her previously published work includes a series of celebrity producer profiles for *Millimeter* magazine and contributions to "Designing Eye," a nationally syndicated newspaper column about decorating trends.

In addition, she has held executive positions in communications, cable television, and the entertainment industry. She and her husband reside in New York City.

Acknowledgments

In the world of interior design, spectacular bedrooms are the result only of a generous collaborative effort, and the same is true for this book. I would like to express my sincerest gratitude to the very talented interior designers and photographers who were kind enough to share their work and insights, and my deep thanks to the distinguished men and women who were gracious enough to allow us all a glimpse into their bedrooms and private spaces.

My very special thanks to: Mark J. Estren, for his brilliant input; to Mia Amato, Bernice Stone, Craig Smyth, Kathy Rosenblatt, Audrey Molinari, Ivan Dolin, Carolyn London, David Hochberg, Doreen Salerno, James Blakely III, and Mario Buatta for their generous support, and expertise; to my wonderful agents Marilyn Allen and Bob Diforio, who guided me so well; to my editor extraordinaire Paula Munier and my very talented assistant editor Wendy Simard; and to the photography and production geniuses including Betsy Gammons, Regina Grenier, Jen Hornsby, Kristy Mulkern, Francine Hornberger, David Martinell, and to all the other lovely people at Rockport Publishers for their unflagging enthusiasm, clear vision, dedication, and support throughout.

My deepest gratitude goes to the following people for their love and support: Martha Bermont, Rose Dannay, Phil, Jane, Stephen and Carrie Dossick, Rose, Arthur, Peggy, Ron and Christina Doster, Susan and Sandy Diamond, Nancy Edwards, José Cabrera, David Kellman, Rose Marie Tango, Arlene and Tom Buckley, William F. Megevick, Jr., Kate and Dick Oliver, Julie Jackson, Richard and Teresa Conlon, Marcia Lara, Shepard Goldman, Pat Conner, Joan Burger, Douglas Vlachos, Al Goldstein, Barbara Cortese, Don Roosa, Laurance LaCause, Paul McKeon, Jack and Shirley McLeod, Reza Asef, Steffi Wilson, Mark Ritchie, Dick Barlow, Aton Edwards, Ginger Davis, Jimmy Arauz, Adele Stroh, Steve and Erin Reardon, Dale Carey, and Ann Robbins.

And, thanks above all to my beloved husband, Jeffrey, whose patience, generosity of spirit, and loving encouragement helped me to realize my dream.